Everyone is searching for love, but many are [looking in the wrong] places. Pastor Jarrid Wilson has written a life[-changing book, Love Is] Oxygen. In this gospel-centered book, Jarrid [skillfully and lovingly] leads the reader on a journey to know and ex[perience the unbroken,] unequalled, and unmatched love of God revealed through his Son. When you get to know God intimately, you will realize that love isn't something God does; love is who God is. Read this book now.

CRAIG GROESCHEL
Senior pastor of Life.Church and author of *Divine Direction: 7 Decisions That Will Change Your Life*

Jarrid will help you catch your breath and discover how to inhale more hope, more healing, more Jesus in your life.

MARGARET FEINBERG
Author of *Fight Back with Joy*

Jarrid Wilson is more than just a compelling writer; he is also a compelling human being. I know this because I am privileged to call this gifted, lovely young man my friend. In these pages, Jarrid gives us a window into his life, where we see him being transformed by the Love about which he writes. This, of course, is what makes his message credible. As you read, I trust that you will come to love God and others more deeply. You will probably also find yourself wanting to become a better person. Thank you, Jarrid, for such a beautiful and compelling book.

SCOTT SAULS
Senior pastor of Christ Presbyterian Church in Nashville, Tennessee, and author of *Jesus Outside the Lines* and *Befriend*

In *Love Is Oxygen*, Jarrid Wilson cuts through the noise of today and points us to what matters most—the extravagant and inexhaustible love of God. To know God's love is the journey we are all created to be on. Encountering the depth and height of God's love is a lifelong discovery that will continue throughout eternity. God's love for you is so extravagant that it can be hard to comprehend, but it is so easily available for those willing to receive it. Jarrid so brilliantly articulates the revolutionary truth that Jesus is God's gift of love to us and how that affects every area of our lives. *Love Is Oxygen* is a timely gift for those yearning to know the love of God and grow deeper in their understanding of the great mystery of his love for us. Not only will your life be changed, but as you give God's love away, those around you will also be transformed.

BANNING LIEBSCHER
Founder and pastor of Jesus Culture

Why is it the simplest tenets of the faith are the hardest to realize and live? I'm grateful for the unwavering truths Jarrid Wilson shares in *Love Is Oxygen* because they remind me of this settled fact: I am loved, and it is God who does the loving. Succinct, heartfelt, and full of real-life stories, Wilson's book will empower Christ followers to live and breathe and move within the powerful grasp of God's love.

MARY DEMUTH
Author of more than thirty books, including *Worth Living: How God's Wild Love for You Makes You Worthy*

When Jarrid says that "love is oxygen," he means it, but beyond simple love, it's the honesty he writes with that will encourage you the most. He puts it all on the page, and his refusal to clean up the messy parts, to polish the prose until his pride is protected, is what makes this book so good.

JON ACUFF
New York Times bestselling author of *Do Over*

What I love about this book is how Jarrid lets you under the surface and reveals his real story. He not only shares his vulnerability but also speaks passionately of Jesus. We all need Jesus more than we realize. *Love Is Oxygen* brings us closer to him and helps us see Jesus more clearly.

DANIEL FUSCO
Lead pastor of Crossroads Community Church and author of *Upward, Inward, Outward* and *Honestly*

Jarrid's vulnerability and honesty will quickly capture the hearts of those who have ever struggled with depression or with simply being overwhelmed. The victory and overcoming principle of love will serve as refreshment for all.

DR. JOHNNY M. HUNT
Author of *Demolishing Strongholds*

Throughout this book, Jarrid's brutal honesty inherently highlights the greatness of God's love. His writing reminds me of Paul's teachings on boasting only about our weaknesses.

JOEY SVENDSEN
Pastor and host of the *BadChristian* podcast

In a world of divisiveness and negativity, Jarrid Wilson is convinced that your life can burst with kindness and grace. But it's Wilson's authenticity, not optimism, that makes this book sing. Wilson tears open his chest and drains his beating heart onto every page, sharing raw stories of what love looks like in real time. Do not read this book if you're content inhaling the stale air of our pessimistic age—because one whiff of *Love Is Oxygen* will force you to love bigger, broader, and better than ever before.

JONATHAN MERRITT
Contributing writer for the *Atlantic* and author of *Learning to Speak God from Scratch*

Jarrid Wilson is one of the most genuinely loving men of God I know. His ability to communicate gospel truths in a fresh and biblical way perfectly positions him to stir you to something you've never experienced and to also change your view of God and people. This book is going to feel like a breath of fresh air for your spirit.

JOSH HOWERTON
Lead pastor of The Bridge Church, Spring Hill, Tennessee

Jarrid Wilson writes with simple grace about how love rises from the ashes of depression. He reminds us all how God is love, and so as we love others through our actions, we are loving God. As you read, you will want to grab hold of the ever-present opportunities to act out of love and discover life.

BECCA STEVENS
Founder and president of Thistle Farms

Jarrid Wilson writes with great clarity and openness about the remarkable love of God. He shares his story so transparently and points all of us to the greatest love of all. *Love Is Oxygen* is inspiration, application, challenge, and encouragement in one remarkable book.

JUD WILHITE
Senior pastor of Central Church and author of *Pursued*

Some people just see things differently. Jarrid Wilson is one of those people. Just when you think you've heard everything there is to hear about love, you encounter Jarrid. I'm so grateful for Jarrid's voice—it challenges me.

CAREY NIEUWHOF
Author and founding pastor of Connexus Church, Ontario, Canada

Battling with depression, anxiety, and loneliness is something many of us face at some point in our lives. Jarrid does an amazing job at shining light into the depths of hurt and confusion, while resting in what truly matters.

CHELSEA CROCKETT
Author of *Your Own Beautiful*

All our lives we've heard the phrase "God is love" without any real understanding of what it actually means or its implications for our lives. Now, Jarrid Wilson's new book, *Love Is Oxygen*, takes everything we thought we knew about love and turns it on its head. For anyone who has ever struggled with love or being loved, for anyone who thinks God is a hard taskmaster, or perhaps most important, for anyone who thinks love is nice, clean, and G-rated, this book is for you. You'll never look at love the same way again.

PHIL COOKE
Filmmaker, media consultant, and author of *One Big Thing: Discovering What You Were Born to Do*

There are positive people who make you laugh and feel better about yourself. And then there are "hope dealers," who offer something much deeper. Jarrid Wilson writes about a hope not born of this world, but in a loving Father. Your very soul will be encouraged by this book.

MICHAEL LUKASZEWSKI
Founder of Church Fuel

It's been said that we accept only the love we think we deserve. This book will expand your potential to accept the empowerment of God's great love.

KEVIN GERALD
Lead pastor of Champions Centre and author of *Good Things*

God knew the world needed a huge dose of gracious encouragement, so he sent Jarrid Wilson into it. His writings continue to nudge me, and so many others, toward choosing to show relentless love instead of reactive judgment. *Love Is Oxygen* is one of those must-reads for every believer—and every skeptic, too! We all need to breathe this in deeply!

BRANDON COX

Lead pastor of Grace Hills Church in Bentonville, Arkansas, author, and leadership coach

This book is exactly what the world needs today. From the very first page, Jarrid takes you deep inside his soul and shows us all how God's unfailing love can take us from broken to beautiful.

JASON ROMANO

Former ESPN producer and current host of the *Sports Spectrum* podcast

My dear friend Jarrid reminds us of the truest truth in the universe: that God loves us. Undeniably, irrevocably, unashamedly. God's love is fierce—fiercer than the pain and wreckage of this life, as terrifying as they can be. And believing in and receiving this mind-boggling love of God changes everything about our lives. This book contains the message that can shake the church and the world upside down. This book is gold.

MATT BROWN (@EVANGELISTMATT)

Evangelist, author, and founder of Think Eternity

From his very first sentence, Jarrid boldly shares his journey to embrace God's love and share it with others. Filled with trademark vulnerability and biblical examples, *Love Is Oxygen* points us to God's love—our deepest need and most powerful resource. If you roll your eyes when you hear about God's love, you need to pick up this book!

SCOTT SAVAGE

Lead pastor of Cornerstone Church in Prescott, Arizona, author, and writer at ScottSavageLive.com

Jarrid Wilson does a brilliant job of helping us discover the power of God's love and how it can transform every area of our lives. His transparency and authenticity will draw you in, and you will experience a life-giving relationship with God.

MATT FRY

Lead pastor of C3 Church in Clayton, North Carolina, and author of *I Am*

Breathe in the power of Jarrid's words! They are his honest and human pursuit to discover what God's love truly meant for him and what it will mean for you. Fantastic read!

STEVE CARTER

Teaching pastor at Willow Creek Community Church and author of *This Invitational Life*

Jarrid Wilson has done it again! In a world filled with sound bites, *Love Is Oxygen* offers so much more! He offers an encouraging yet challenging opportunity to breathe in the love of Jesus so that we can breathe it out to a world desperately in need of the love only Jesus can provide. *Love Is Oxygen* is more than a breath of fresh air. It's a call to action! It's a call to receive love but also to live love. I want to answer that call!

PASTOR J. R. LEE

Founder and lead pastor of Freedom Church

As long as I've known Jarrid Wilson, I've been impressed with his raw vulnerability and willingness to blaze a trail down a road most are too fearful to venture, bringing light to the valley of the shadow of death. During my NFL career, the place of darkness I found myself in was excruciatingly lonely. Far too many of us have bought the lie we need to look the part. Suck it up. Have it all together. Publicly performing, while privately dying. *Love Is Oxygen* will fill your heart with hope and awaken courage you always possessed but never saw—until now.

CLINT GRESHAM

Author of *Becoming*, Super Bowl XLVIII winner, and international speaker

The best books are the ones written from our own understanding—the sacred place of wrestle, lack, and hope. Jarrid Wilson has fought for every insight in *Love Is Oxygen*, and it shows. I appreciate the honest, tender truth presented in the pages and the straightforward lessons the reader can easily glean for life application. Good work, Jarrid. May this book be the healing balm and teaching tool you penned.

LISA WHITTLE
Speaker and author of *I Want God*

Jarrid, your willingness to bare all about your experience with depression will bring help and healing to many souls. Thank you for reminding us all that even when we feel like God has failed us, his heart beats relentlessly with love toward us. This is a wonderful book!

JAY HAIZLIP
Founder and senior pastor of The Sanctuary Church in Los Angeles and cast member of *Preachers of L.A.*

In *Love Is Oxygen*, Jarrid Wilson displays an impressive level of vulnerability that is both refreshing and disarming to the reader. This book provides a Christ-focused, hope-filled response to many weighty issues that confront our culture today.

CURTIS ZACKERY
Pastor and author of *Soul Rest*

Jarrid's authenticity and transparency are so refreshing! *Love Is Oxygen* is one of those books you can give to anyone and it will impact them! My friend Jarrid Wilson is such a kind and refreshing person. His story of brokenness and pain is a powerful testimony of God's love. I believe this book will help many see God's true heart toward them!

JASON KIMBROW
Pastor at New Life Church in Fayetteville, Arkansas

Love Is Oxygen engages us on a journey of rediscovery. Jared's insight, transparency, and personal experiences are seamlessly woven throughout the threads of this book perfectly. If you desire to read and learn more about God's love and his designed path for your life, this book will not disappoint.

TIM TIMBERLAKE

Lead pastor of Christian Faith Center in Creedmoor, North Carolina, and author of *Abandon*

When you read *Love Is Oxygen*, you'll learn a lot about authenticity, redemption, and love . . . I did. Jarrid's story will intersect with yours because we all have a bit of bottled brokenness in us.

DAVE STONE

Pastor at Southeast Christian Church in Louisville, Kentucky

Love Is Oxygen is showing up in our world at exactly the right time. In my forty years of living, I'm not sure I can remember a time when LOVE was more needed. Love for one another but also love for ourselves: the kind of love that only God can supply. I'm thankful for Jarrid Wilson sharing his story with us and helping us see the transformational power of love.

TYLER REAGIN

President of Catalyst Leader

Love Is Oxygen is more than a book; it's a road map to a new beginning for anyone who has ever felt heartbroken, hopeless, or just tired of trying. No matter where you are in your journey, this book's powerful truths and inspiring stories will infuse your heart with encouragement and renewed faith. This book will change your perspective, and in doing so, it might just change your life.

DAVE WILLIS

Pastor and bestselling author of *The Seven Laws of Love*

Jarrid's message of love is real and palpable. I was reminded of all the years I spent able to take in only shallow breaths of God's love for me—and how wonderful it was when I was finally able to breathe him in fully. If you have wondered about God's love for you or about how to better love those around you, read this book.

ANNA LEBARON

Author of *The Polygamist's Daughter*

LOVE *is* OXYGEN

L O V E
is O X Y G E N

---

*How God Can Give You Life
and Change Your World*

JARRID WILSON

A NavPress resource published in alliance
with Tyndale House Publishers, Inc.

NavPress is the publishing ministry of The Navigators, an international Christian organization and leader in personal spiritual development. NavPress is committed to helping people grow spiritually and enjoy lives of meaning and hope through personal and group resources that are biblically rooted, culturally relevant, and highly practical.

For more information, visit www.NavPress.com.

Love Is Oxygen: How God Can Give You Life and Change Your World

Copyright © 2017 by Jarrid Wilson. All rights reserved.

A NavPress resource published in alliance with Tyndale House Publishers, Inc.

NAVPRESS and the NAVPRESS logo are registered trademarks of NavPress, The Navigators, Colorado Springs, CO. *TYNDALE* is a registered trademark of Tyndale House Publishers, Inc. Absence of ® in connection with marks of NavPress or other parties does not indicate an absence of registration of those marks.

The Team:
Don Pape, Publisher
Caitlyn Carlson, Acquisitions Editor
Helen Macdonald, Copyeditor
Eva Winters, Designer

Cover photograph of bubbles copyright © by Anthony Harrison/Lightstock. All rights reserved.
Cover photograph of water by Tim Marshall/Unsplash.com. All rights reserved.

Published in association with the literary agency of Wolgemuth & Associates, Inc.

Unless otherwise indicated, all Scripture quotations are taken from the *Holy Bible*, New Living Translation, copyright © 1996, 2004, 2015 by Tyndale House Foundation. Used by permission of Tyndale House Publishers, Inc., Carol Stream, Illinois 60188. All rights reserved. Scripture quotations marked ESV are taken from *The Holy Bible*, English Standard Version® (ESV®), copyright © 2001 by Crossway, a publishing ministry of Good News Publishers. Used by permission. All rights reserved. Scripture quotations marked MSG are taken from *THE MESSAGE*, copyright © 1993, 1994, 1995, 1996, 2000, 2001, 2002 by Eugene H. Peterson. Used by permission of NavPress. All rights reserved. Represented by Tyndale House Publishers, Inc. Scripture quotations marked NIV are taken from the Holy Bible, *New International Version*,® *NIV*® Copyright © 1973, 1978, 1984, 2011 by Biblica, Inc.® Used by permission. All rights reserved worldwide.

Some of the anecdotal illustrations in this book are true to life and are included with the permission of the persons involved. All other illustrations are composites of real situations, and any resemblance to people living or dead is purely coincidental.

For information about special discounts for bulk purchases, please contact Tyndale House Publishers at csresponse@tyndale.com, or call 1-800-323-9400.

Cataloging-in-Publication Data is available.

ISBN 978-1-63146-760-8

Printed in the United States of America

23	22	21	20	19	18	17
7	6	5	4	3	2	1

To Juli, my wife and best friend.

You have no idea how much I love and appreciate you. Your love for God, our children, and the world around you encourages me daily.

CONTENTS

Chapter 1

———

DISCOVER
the WONDER

There I was, sitting in my light tan 1997 Toyota 4Runner, googling "painless ways to commit suicide." I was broken, empty, full of hatred toward God, and severely depressed. I felt as if I were drowning. I had made my way up to an area known as Skyline, just outside my suburban residence in Southern California, and had parked on the edge of a cliff that overlooked the entire county. To my right was San Diego, and to my left was Los Angeles. Two beautiful cities, and I was between them, overwhelmed by darkness and hopelessness.

I never thought I'd reach this point. I didn't love myself, and I didn't love my life or anything about it. Growing up, I'd had an answer for just about everything, but now I couldn't get my head around what was happening. I didn't know where to go.

I was standing in front of a spiritual blockade. God's love seemed blatantly absent in my life, and my heart was like a dried-up well. I felt as though I was alone in the corner while the rest of the world passed by without noticing me. And I was searching for life in all the wrong places: in the party scene, in drugs, and in relationships. Anything that kept me from feeling lonely and worthless. I was yearning for hope, but shallow realities were giving me none of it.

I know I'm not alone. A lot of us have been there before, in that place where everything just seems to fall to pieces.

I was twenty years old and trying to figure out where I fit in the world. I wanted to love God, but I just didn't know how. The people around me who claimed to have a relationship with God seemed full of joy and hope. Something was different about them. They were excited to go to church on Sundays, liked to read their Bibles, and lifted their hands during worship. I saw what they had and wanted that for myself.

I wanted a relationship with Jesus. But I just didn't know where to start. I wanted to find forgiveness for my sins. But I just didn't know what to do. I wanted to be used by God. But I just didn't know how to ask. Being full of God's love wasn't as easy as pastors and Sunday school teachers had made it out to be.

Because of my depression, I believed the lie that nobody in the world, least of all God, would blink an eye if I were gone. And that my brokenness was too big a burden for even God to bear. No amount of Zoloft could keep me from feeling down. No amount of counseling sessions could keep me from thinking I was worthless. And no amount of truth could keep me from believing the lies I repeatedly told myself. I was my own worst enemy, and I seemed to be very good at defeating myself daily. I was ready to say good-bye to everything I had known in life—which was right where Satan wanted me. It was a frightening place to be.

Maybe I was depressed because of the sports injury that almost led to my leg being amputated during my sophomore year of high school and completely destroyed my chances of playing professional soccer. Or maybe it was because I had found out that I had a rare blood disorder resembling leukemia and was only days away from starting chemotherapy. I assume my feelings of worthlessness had more to do with the fact that I had been digging my feet in the sand in an attempt to hold back God from my life. I think I was just scared of fully committing my life to someone. And I couldn't find a way to keep joy within my life, no matter how hard I tried. I felt like a kite without wind, a river without a current. Everything seemed useless, and I blamed God for what I was feeling. Even though I wouldn't have called myself a fully devoted follower of Jesus, I still figured God would see my pain and agony and do something about it.

The thing is, he was giving me all the answers I needed. I just wasn't listening.

Sometimes what we perceive as God being silent is actually our sin and selfishness keeping us from turning an ear to his voice. As the Bible says in Jeremiah 1:5, God had been speaking to me before he had formed me in the womb—his voice echoed with truth before any of us had been formed. But I'd been choosing a life that relied solely on my own strength, desires, and schedule. For us to fully grab hold of God-centered lives, we have to be willing to let go of our self-centered ones.

The Unexpected Rescue

I'd heard the phrase "God is love" plenty of times, but I never really took it to heart. After all, "God is love" seemed to contradict the way in which some Christians had treated me and others. I was never good enough for them, never acted holy enough, and didn't look the way a supposedly "good Christian" was supposed to look. I was a misfit. But I realize now that God specializes in the utilization of misfits.

It was the darkest time of my life, and I was tired of hearing about the love of God from friends and family members. I didn't care who God was or what he had done for me. I wanted results—tangible results I could find hope in. And I blamed God for how I felt. Why couldn't he take this pain away? Why couldn't he help me? Why couldn't he have kept me from experiencing the things that led me down this dark road?

Depression has a way of making you blind to everything true. It's a blockade that keeps you from feeling anything other than complete darkness. It's something millions of people struggle with, and—sadly—suicide was the tenth leading cause of death in the United States in 2013, and it's the second leading cause of death for people between the ages of fifteen and thirty-four.[1]

I know not everyone in this world has dealt with depression or anxiety, but I'm 100 percent certain that you've felt broken, lonely, and hopeless at one time or another. Love and acceptance were nowhere to be found. You felt as though you weren't good enough. God seemed absent.

Maybe right now you feel "just okay," and that is actually the best you've felt in a very long time. Your brokenness traps you because of things that happened in your past. Things you wish had never taken place. Maybe they're regrets or failures.

Or perhaps you've yet to let go and find peace amid the violent storm of your worst memories—the ones you've tried to lock up in your closet. The ones you don't like people knowing about. You're hurting. You're frustrated. You're in repetitious, unwavering pain. You ask yourself, *Does God even care?* I've asked that question. I've been in that place far too many times.

The beautiful reality is that God *does* care about you. And he cares about me. God loves us. He feels your pain. He feels my pain. And while he sometimes responds to us in a way that might not be exactly how we anticipate, it doesn't mean he hasn't heard our cries. He cares—deeply—about our pain and yearning for hope. I wish I could go back in time and tell myself that. Oh, the sorrow I could have avoided! But then again, I believe God works everything out for a reason.

I'm reminded of a passage in the Bible that illustrates so beautifully the uncertainty of our hearts:

> We don't yet see things clearly. We're squinting
> in a fog, peering through a mist. But it won't be
> long before the weather clears and the sun shines

> bright! We'll see it all then, see it all as clearly
> as God sees us, knowing him directly just as he
> knows us!
>
> I CORINTHIANS 13:12, MSG

Though we sometimes wonder what is happening in our lives, and though we cannot see clearly what lies ahead or know which direction to take, we have this hope: God promises that he will clear the storms and give us direction. He sees us, and he will bring us out of the haze we find ourselves in.

Over the course of my life, I've found myself furious at God on multiple occasions. Why? Because I'm human. I've yelled at God, cursed at God, and even threatened God because he wasn't providing what I felt was the best response for my current situation. As if my feeble and frail threats had any impact on his decisions. You and I are but specks compared to his majesty and greatness.

I'm sure he looked at me patiently, waiting for me to finish my rant, and knew that I didn't really mean what I was saying. I was just upset, broken, and frustrated beyond belief. He knew I wasn't yet accepting the love he had for me. I was too blind to see it. But in God's grace and patience, he allowed me to vent to him. He allowed me to use him as a punching bag. That's an aspect of the beauty of God—he's big enough to handle anything I throw at him but wise enough to not give me everything I ask for. A loving Father at his finest.

You might think God is unfair for not giving you all you

desire, but in reality it's quite the opposite. It's not God's job to live up to our personal expectations. God's will is not dependent on our wants. He does what he knows is in our best interest and for his glory. Our job is to trust him through the process, no matter how hard it might be.

That's easier said than done, I know. But when you learn to truly let go of yourself and instead grab hold of what God has laid out for you, life will begin to make a lot more sense. A sense of purpose and identity will come over you, increasing your yearning to pursue him that much more. God's love is available to all of us, no matter where we're from, what we look like, or what we've done. God's love is for anyone who calls upon him for life and hope.

When you put your life in God's hands, you must trust him fully, even when you don't understand what he's doing, why he's doing it, and for how long. Some things have only one answer: Trust God even when it doesn't make sense. Trusting God in the midst of your brokenness is a beautifully painful but spiritually deepening experience. Every time you put your trust in God, another scoop of your self-obsession is removed and replaced with the righteousness of God.

You must trust God with your brokenness but realize it's okay to be mad at him, frustrated, and even downright confused. He can handle it. God doesn't expect you to understand everything he does. You can question what's happening. You can wave your fist a little. You don't have to act as if you have it all together. God can handle it. He wants you to let it all out and be honest with him about what you're really feeling.

When you give God the room he deserves, your soul finds supernatural refreshment and peace in his presence. After all, we were created for the partnership of God. We were created to do life hand in hand with the one who created us in his image. God's love is in the business of rescuing those who feel as though they're suffocating, though he often acts in ways we don't expect. But it's still love, and we desperately need it.

Chapter 2

LOVE *is*
the ANSWER

The day on the cliff, as I sat in the car my mother and father had lovingly given me a few years earlier, I tried so hard to convince myself that life was worth living, that there was something out there actually worth fighting for. I mean, isn't that the question we yearn to have answered? To know what on earth we are here for?

My attempts at convincing myself of my value in life continued to fail me. Would people care if I were gone? Would a world without me really be any different? I thought ending it all was easier than admitting my brokenness to others—let alone God. I didn't want to admit that I felt as though God had abandoned me. After all, I grew up in a Christian home. I grew up in church. I attended youth group every week, memorized Bible verses, and even made sure to pray before I went to bed. I wasn't supposed to feel like this. I must be broken. I must not be good enough for the wondrous life that God had given to so many others.

Growing up, I believed Christians weren't supposed to be broken. I'd never heard a pastor tell me he felt faithless, made mistakes, or was going through tough times. I'm not saying those pastors don't exist; I had just never heard one admit those things. So I was left thinking that if I felt these things, I was a bad Christian and must be doing something wrong. It's as if you never saw your parents argue when you were a kid, so when you get married and start arguing with your spouse, you think something is wrong with your own marriage (not realizing that your parents actually *did* argue, just not in front of you).

So what did I do? I bottled up all my brokenness and pretended as though everything was just dandy. I didn't want anyone to know how I was really feeling. I don't recommend doing this. When you hold things inside, it's very similar to putting a pack of Mentos in a two-liter bottle of Diet Coke: You're eventually going to explode, and your mess is going to affect everyone around you.

All of us can be a little like the airplanes my grandfather and I saw at an aviation show. He and I had enjoyed look-ing at some of the last century's most memorable airplanes, which were carefully restored and in pristine condition . . . or so we thought. The engines and interiors told another story. Most of the planes didn't fly, lacked complete engines, or had interiors straight out of the apocalypse. The planes had looked perfect from afar, but in reality, they were far from perfect.

In our obsession with social media, we love to paint the persona of perfection. We try to present flawless exteri-ors, desperately hoping our windows are tinted enough so nobody can see what things really look like on the inside.

It's similar to when Jesus called out the Pharisees and scribes for cleaning the outside of the cup and dish but leaving the inside disgusting and vile (see Matthew 23:25). We're not fooling anybody, and the reality is that we're doing more harm to ourselves than good.

Prior to that day on the cliff, I constantly found myself trying to act as though I had it all together—as if I had all the answers. I thought the more I had my life together, the more people would respect me. I couldn't have been more wrong. Living like this meant I wasn't going to let anyone know I was hurting. No way was I going to show any type of weakness that could possibly make me look bad in front of others.

But while the image I was portraying might have looked flawless and pristine, the interior of my soul was ravaged, hurting, and seeking worth in the approval of others. I wasn't really who I pretended to be, and it was exhausting trying to keep up appearances.

From the outside looking in, people probably thought I was fine. Nobody would have guessed that I was feeling so much pain at such a young age. I had a loving family, big goals, all the encouragement I could ask for, and a great group of friends. But no one knew that I'd been struggling with this hurt for the last five years of my life. I hid that I was taking medication because I was too embarrassed to admit it. I was in way over my head, and I wasn't looking to deal with it any longer. I was ready to finally let go and make the pain stop once and for all.

Maybe you're in that same spot right now. Or maybe you know someone who is. But you need to know this: It's okay to not have it all together. None of us do. That's the reason God sent Jesus, a gift of love. It's okay to not have all the answers. And it's okay to admit to others that you need help. I don't have it all together, but the beauty of it is that I do have God in my life. He loves me despite all my shortcomings and failures. He loves *you* despite all your shortcomings and failures.

There's freedom in admitting we're not perfect. We must allow ourselves to be human, make mistakes, and break the bondage that comes from constantly portraying perfection. We're not perfect and we never will be (on this earth). Don't feel pressured to be anything other than who God has called you to be. Ignore the opinions of others. Reflect an honest and authentic version of yourself each and every day. Everyone has a highlight reel, but we also all have outtakes.

While crying out to God that day in my car, my face covered in sweat and tears, I felt overwhelmed. And then at the moment I felt at the end of it all, my screams of "I can't do this anymore, God" were met with a sense of his presence, a presence that words cannot begin to describe. I thought I might be psyching myself out a bit, overspiritualizing this whole thing, but I quickly realized how real this actually was. I had dropped my pride, broken down the walls, admitted I was powerless on my own, and I was looking to embrace something bigger than myself: God. And when those walls fell, he was there on the other side, waiting, ready to embrace me with his all-encompassing love.

As I continued to try to share my anger with the one who had created me, I noticed my voice slowly lowering in volume, my anger starting to cease, my racing heart beginning to slow down. God finally interrupted my cries and said, "Give me a chance." It was a voice that had no sound but echoed throughout my veins. It startled me and comforted me at the same time.

"But, God, I don't want to feel like this anymore!" I shouted, tears streaming down my face.

His response was something I have never forgotten: "Jarrid, I don't want you to feel like this anymore either."

That was the moment when God wrecked my life in the most incredible way imaginable. It was as though a semi-truck had slammed into the innermost place of my heart. His words were so simple yet so powerful at the same time. In an instant, I felt as though I had discovered the wonder of God's love for me. This was an encounter like no other. His love became tangible, evident—something I could truly feel within. God yearned for me to embrace his love and share his love, a love filled with hope, a purpose, and a destiny unlike anything else in this world. For the first time in my life, I knew God saw me. He had always seen me. He had always cared. I could breathe again. My soul was filled. My heart took flight.

Many of us have experienced this—that moment when

God steps in, speaks up, calls our attention to what he's doing in our lives. The truth is that we've all seen a demonstration of God's love. Romans 1:20 states,

> Ever since the world was created, people have seen the earth and sky. Through everything God made, they can clearly see his invisible qualities—his eternal power and divine nature. So they have no excuse for not knowing God.

But discovering the love of God is what will truly bring us into a personal relationship with him. It's life altering, to say the least. Something came over me that I couldn't describe. It was almost an out-of-body experience.

I was encountering everything I had ever hoped for in terms of biblical faith, and it was the beginning of what I call my "discovery moment"—the moment when someone comes to discover the wonder of God's love in a way that transforms him or her from the inside out. Life-altering love. The kind of love you cannot help but shout from the rooftops and bring up in every conversation, and you can't hold back a smile when thinking about it.

I believe all of us have the opportunity to have a God-altering discovery in our lives. I mean everyone: you, me, the guy working at the gas station, the all-star athlete, the addict, the lady at the bar, the porn star, the news anchor on television, all ten of the kids playing basketball at the local park, your abusive parent, and even your crazy neighbor. All of us have the opportunity to discover the wonder of God's transformative love. I believe this is true because God created us for this love—because he is love and we were created in his image. Discovering the wonder of this love brings us change and extraordinary truth. The irony of the Christian life is that the more we realize how lost we truly are without God's love, the more fulfillment we can actually find in Christ. God's love can open the door to life—true and exuberant life. A life that takes all our senses into consideration and brings us to new levels of spiritual understanding.

For me, the years following this encounter with God were full of ups and downs, victories and defeats—but everything had changed, because now, every moment, I know God is with me. No matter what I go through, I can see it as part of the story God is writing in my heart. God can take anyone from anywhere and, through his love, do wonderful and magnificent things.

God Loves Your Story

I don't know if I will ever be able to say I'm proud of the person I was before I came into a loving relationship with God, but I can say without a shadow of doubt that God loves my story because it's helped shape and mold me into who I am today. I know God loves your story too. God loves us so much that he can take any part of our lives—broken, beautiful, and everything in between—and use it for the glory of his name. My past of depression, loneliness, and pain has allowed me to connect with people around the world with the same struggles. I wasn't always open about my past and my continuous battle for mental health, but I've quickly learned that the more open I am about it, the more God can use it—and in turn help me continue to fight.

The reality is I might not ever fully conquer the product of sin that is depression, but I do know that God has given me the strength and hope to rise above what depression wants me to think of myself. I realize I might not ever be able to fully step away from medication or counseling, and that's okay too. Anyone who tells you otherwise is wrong. There's nothing in the Bible that says we shouldn't combat sickness and pain using the medical advancements that have emerged from the minds of people made in the image of God. I believe Jesus alone has the power to heal any sickness or ailment in this world, and does so often, but I also understand this doesn't mean he's definitely going to do it for me. We wouldn't tell a cancer patient to lay off the chemotherapy and instead focus on God, so why would we say that to someone who's seeking mental wellness? Now, I'm not saying everyone who suffers needs medication, because that's not the case. That's between you, God, and the respected counsel of a pastor and a licensed psychiatrist. They all work hand in hand to help you. But what I am saying is this: Don't think taking medication and seeking professional help mean that you are weak or a bad

Christian. Because it's not true. Medication is not the enemy of faith. And it's okay to not be okay.

Depression is a part of my story, and it's a hard part of my story. But here's the thing about the hardships we face: As we understand and learn to live in the love of God, our stories can become a way of spreading that love to others. I recently spoke at a Christian festival where a few thousand people were listening to their favorite bands, worshiping together, and visiting the many tents that housed different organizations. I had the opportunity to speak twice over the four days, and one session was about three times more crowded than the other. The session was titled "Depression and Light," and I was going to share about my battle with mental health, with the goal of giving hope to those who maybe felt ashamed to admit they were struggling too. The room was packed, and people were sitting on the floor and in their chairs with pen and paper in hand. I felt a bit intimidated because I felt the weight of the situation: People who were struggling were waiting to hear if I had something to say that could help them.

My plan was to discuss a chapter in the book of Job, a book full of one man's tension between darkness and light, explaining that even some of God's brightest saints have dealt with the darkest of depression and mental illness. Job, Jonah, Abraham, and David are just a few of the men of God who suffered greatly with darkness in their lives, but they all came out on top. They all found comfort and protection in God's love.

As I walked up to the microphone to open the session in

prayer, I felt God tell me to do something I hadn't planned. I questioned him for a second, and then I remembered something my wife had always told me: *"Give people the gift of going second."* If I was going to be authentic with these people about my struggles, then I should be fully honest with them—no holding back. There was no such thing as being "kind of" authentic. So I listened to God. With hundreds of eyes watching me, I walked over to my backpack and then said to the crowd, "I'm going to do something I didn't plan on doing this morning." I took out my antidepressant medication, twisted off the top, and said, "I want you to know that you're not alone. And to show you that I'm in need of a Savior just as much as you are, I'd like to ask your permission to take my antidepressant in front of all of you. Is that okay?"

Cheers of "Yes!" and "Amen!" filled the room. I popped my little white pill into my mouth, washed it down with a swig from a bottle of water, and said, "Okay, now let's talk real life when it comes to depression and mental health." To my surprise, people started to stand up and cheer. Not because I had taken an antidepressant, but because I was 100 percent honest with them. I wasn't trying to hide my struggle. My wife calls this the gift of going second, when you can show people your pain and baggage and give them the freedom to let down their guard and talk real life with you. You're letting them know your story first so they don't feel as though they have to have it all together with you.

We've all got things in our lives that we struggle with. But the reality is God loves us despite our struggles, and he yearns for us to lean into his love while we fight the hard things in our lives. Above all, God's love is an anthem of hope for our lives. As Romans 8:28 (ESV) says,

> We know that for those who love God all things work together for good, for those who are called according to his purpose.

No matter what your story is—whether it involves depression or divorce or fear or doubt—God loves it because it's yours. And he loves you despite how dark that story might be. The love of God can take your story and mold it into a message that has the power to change the lives of those who hear it. Not because of you but because of what God can and will do through you.

You see, love is like oxygen. It's essential for the Christian life. We can't live without it. We can't breathe without it. And here's the thing about breathing: It gives us life, but holding our breath won't do any good. There's a rhythm to it. We breathe in, and we breathe out. God's love isn't meant to be held in; it's something we exhale to the world around us. We can't help it. That's just how we breathe.

Chapter 3

_____

G O D *is* L O V E

You might be thinking, *Okay, Jarrid, it's great that God loves you. And it's great that you had this life-changing experience. But I haven't had that experience. How do I know that God loves* me? I get that question. I do. I remember asking it many times myself. And in a lot of ways, there's nothing I can tell you that's going to convince you that God loves you. Each of us has to discover that for ourselves. But here's what I can tell you: God's love for you—and for me and for every person ever created—is what the Bible is all about. And when it comes to knowing and understanding the love of God, his Word is a good place to start.

From the very beginning, God has relentlessly loved the humans he made. In fact, even creating humans at all was an act of love—a desire for relationship so profound and passionate it's hard for us to understand. The act of loving is so integral to God's character that the Bible tells us,

> Dear friends, let us continue to love one another,
> for *love comes from God.* Anyone who loves is
> a child of God and knows God. But *anyone*

who does not love does not know God, for God is
love.

God showed how much he loved us by sending
his one and only Son into the world so that we
might have eternal life through him. *This is real
love—not that we loved God, but that he loved us
and sent his Son as a sacrifice to take away our sins.*

Dear friends, since God loved us that much,
we surely ought to love each other. No one
has ever seen God. But if we love each other,
God lives in us, and his love is brought to full
expression in us.

And God has given us his Spirit as proof that
we live in him and he in us. Furthermore, we have
seen with our own eyes and now testify that the
Father sent his Son to be the Savior of the world.
All who declare that Jesus is the Son of God have
God living in them, and they live in God. *We
know how much God loves us, and we have put our
trust in his love.*

God is love, and all who live in love live in God,
and God lives in them. And as we live in God, our
love grows more perfect. So we will not be afraid
on the day of judgment, but we can face him with
confidence because we live like Jesus here in this
world.

1 JOHN 4:7-17, EMPHASIS ADDED

Do you see what John is saying in this passage? If anyone does not love others, then that person doesn't know God. Why? Because *God is love*. It's that simple. No matter who we are or what we've done, God loves us and wants us to know his love. There's no partiality in his eyes. His love runs rampant and wild. If our lives are without love, then our lives are without God.

I could write this entire book on how we see the reality of God's love in and through all of Scripture. Just look at the book of Exodus. God's people, the Israelites, were slaves in Egypt. Pharaoh feared their numbers—there were so many of them that they could overthrow him! So Pharaoh made slavery a living hell for all the Hebrews.

> The Egyptians made the Israelites their slaves. They appointed brutal slave drivers over them, hoping to wear them down with crushing labor. They forced them to build the cities of Pithom and Rameses as supply centers for the king. But the more the Egyptians oppressed them, the more the Israelites multiplied and spread, and the more alarmed the Egyptians became. So the Egyptians worked the people of Israel without mercy. They made their lives bitter, forcing them to mix mortar and make bricks and do all the work in the fields. They were ruthless in all their demands.
>
> EXODUS 1:11-14

Moses, our not-so-fearless leader in the story, was protected from death as a child, adopted by Pharaoh's daughter, raised as an Egyptian, and then given a crazy revelation from God through a burning bush: God saw the Israelites. He loved them deeply. And he wanted them to be free.

Moses audaciously confronted Pharaoh with God's command to let God's people go. And Pharaoh, who wanted to keep his slaves, ignored all the warnings.

> Moses and Aaron went and spoke to Pharaoh. They told him, "This is what the LORD, the God of Israel, says: Let my people go so they may hold a festival in my honor in the wilderness."
>
> "Is that so?" retorted Pharaoh. "And who is the LORD? Why should I listen to him and let Israel go? I don't know the LORD, and I will not let Israel go."
>
> But Aaron and Moses persisted. "The God of the Hebrews has met with us," they declared. "So let us take a three-day journey into the wilderness so we can offer sacrifices to the LORD our God. If we don't, he will kill us with a plague or with the sword."
>
> Pharaoh replied, "Moses and Aaron, why are you distracting the people from their tasks? Get back to work! Look, there are many of your people in the land, and you are stopping them from their work."
>
> EXODUS 5:1-5

God's love doesn't give up in the face of resistance. He doesn't let the words of man get in the way of his rescue. Real love persists. Real love pursues. And that's exactly what we see God doing in this story.

Freeing the Israelites—and doing it through Moses, who had run away from Egypt and had tried to talk God out of using him—would seem to be a daunting task, an impossible mission. But that's what God does. His wisdom, power, and love take impossible out of the equation. *Nothing* can stand between God and his love for those he calls his own. No man, no power, no army, no sword, no hardship, no enemy.

I'm sure the Israelites had often prayed that God would free them from their bondage. But I wonder how many of them had started to give up. How many of them believed the lie that God didn't love them anymore, that he had abandoned them?

But he didn't abandon them. And he doesn't abandon us either.

God used Moses to continue to speak to Pharaoh after he refused to listen to their request. And as Pharaoh still refused to listen, God acted. Blood, frogs, gnats, flies, diseased livestock, boils, hail, locusts, darkness, and the death of the firstborn (see Exodus 7–11). All of these were part of God's punishment against Pharaoh for not releasing his people. These are the great lengths God will go to show love to his people. These are the lengths he will go to set them free.

After the tenth plague, Pharaoh seemed to have had

enough. In Exodus 12:31 we find him calling for Moses and Aaron during the night:

> "Get out!" he ordered. "Leave my people—and take the rest of the Israelites with you! Go and worship the LORD as you have requested."

Pharaoh had had enough and was willing to let God's people go. And God didn't leave his people there, even at the point of freedom. His love doesn't extend only to the point of our obvious need, because we always need it. God gave the Israelites safe passage through the waters, parting the Red Sea and swallowing up Pharaoh's army within it. Then God gave Moses the law, the way to point people toward God, the way for them to follow him and remain in his ever-present love. Because nothing—not outer forces or inner turmoil, not even our own rebellion—stops God's love.

> Who shall separate us from the love of Christ? Shall trouble or hardship or persecution or famine or nakedness or danger or sword? As it is written:
>
> > "For your sake we face death all day long; we are considered as sheep to be slaughtered."
>
> No, in all these things we are more than conquerors through him who loved us. For I am

> convinced that neither death nor life, neither
> angels nor demons, neither the present nor the
> future, nor any powers, neither height nor depth,
> nor anything else in all creation, will be able to
> separate us from the love of God that is in Christ
> Jesus our Lord.
>
> ROMANS 8:35-39, NIV

God's against-all-odds love for us is just as powerful and pursuing as his love for the Israelites. We are his people. His love never changes. It has no bounds, no fear, and no prerequisites. We will always find ourselves face-to-face with God's love no matter where we find ourselves. He meets us right where we are.

God freeing the Israelites from the hands of Pharaoh is an incredible example of his love for his people. God is in the business of protecting his family and going to extreme lengths to make sure they know they are loved. He is a loving Father constantly loving and pursuing his children. And his ultimate act of love was yet another rescue.

A Crown Full of Thorns

Jesus is God's love embodied. Jesus is God's rescue made flesh. Jesus—his life, his death, his resurrection—is the greatest example of God's love. Just as in Exodus, God sent someone to free his people from bondage. Except this freedom isn't from physical slavery: God sent his one and only Son,

Jesus, to liberate his children from the bondage of sin and brokenness—to free you and me, if we choose to follow him out of the slavery we're in.

> For this is how God loved the world: He gave his one and only Son, so that everyone who believes in him will not perish but have eternal life.
>
> JOHN 3:16

Jesus Christ, our Lord and Savior, was hung on a cross in our place to pay a penalty that he didn't owe. He became one of us, wore a crown of thorns, took our judgment, bore our sins, took nails in his hands, and gave up his life so that we might have the opportunity to find life in him.

You can tell the depth of someone's love by what it costs. Christ's great love cost him his life. This act of love is the definition of love itself: giving up your life for the sake of another.

> There is no greater love than to lay down one's life for one's friends.
>
> JOHN 15:13

With the death and resurrection of Jesus, with the freedom from sin, we see God's character of vibrant love made fully known.

Matthew Henry said,

> The Spirit of God is the Spirit of love. He that
> does not love the image of God in his people,
> has no saving knowledge of God. For it is God's
> nature to be kind, and to give happiness. The law
> of God is love; and all would have been perfectly
> happy, had all obeyed it. The provision of the
> gospel, for the forgiveness of sin, and the salvation
> of sinners, consistently with God's glory and
> justice, shows that God is love.[2]

Let me say it again: God. Is. Love. There is nothing you can do to make God love you any more or any less. He died for you. It is finished. He just loves you.

Does this wreck your mind in the way it does mine? God, the creator of the universe, is the definition of love itself—and he showed this by sacrificing his one and only Son. Mind blowing, if you ask me. Our love for God cannot compare to the love he has for us. We cannot outlove him, outforgive him, or outsmart him. He's just that incredible. God foresaw all the ugly pieces of our lives and still chose to send his Son to die for us. He loved us enough to offer us rescue.

Love is the very reason Jesus' body was brutally broken upon that splintered cross. It's unbeatable, unrestricted, and hands down the greatest attribute of Jesus. God's love will transform the way you see life, and it will radically invade the way you see others. God, Jesus, and the Holy Spirit are the definition of love itself.

God Isn't a Bully

Growing up, I didn't understand this about God's love. Instead, I pictured God as a guardian of good who was always looking to strike me down if I messed up or did something that made him mad. Sadly, I got this version of God from countless sermons by pastors who relied on scare tactics to get their points across. And I was brought face-to-face with this mentality when my aunt took me to my first Christian music festival. Although I was still a little skeptical about God and the whole idea of faith, I was excited about this concert I'd heard about. We pulled up to a baseball stadium where almost forty thousand Christians and non-Christians alike would be taking time to worship, listen to a message, and pray together. I was blown away by the idea. But my excitement and curiosity were quickly dampened by the sight of men, women, and children standing on buckets and yelling at people. As we walked by the growing crowd, some called us "disgusting sinners" while others raised a chant of "Repent and be saved!" The hope of Jesus, which I desperately needed, was lost amid hellfire and brimstone. And this happens way too often.

Now that I understand the love of God, which permeates Scripture and has overtaken my life, I wonder why so many people illustrate God in this way. Does the Bible talk about God's wrath? Yes. But does this mean God is nothing but wrathful, seeking to destroy anything and everything in his way? Nope. Not even close. Never once in my studies have I seen God best represented through shouting and judgment. I can assume this happens because people miss that he's a loving and caring Father. God isn't out to get us, nor is he relentlessly searching for a reason to condemn. In fact, I'd go as far as to say that the last thing he would ever want to do is punish or condemn those he loves. Rather, because he loves us, he doesn't want us to stay in lives that keep us away from him. He has to direct us in the ways of righteousness and truth as according to his Word, the same as any parent has to do with his or her child. His correction is actually a by-product of his love for us. And I believe that just like any child, we can choose to ignore him and walk away from the life and wisdom he has for us—and that choice is what separates us from him. This is not to be confused with walking away from salvation, because that's not what I'm saying here.

But even when we turn our backs, he still offers us his love. He is constantly seeking opportunities to show you and me more love and grace. He's anything but the bully who so many people try to make him out to be. I think many of us need to shift our attention to the love and compassion he has to offer rather than the wrath and punishment that only come to those who are against him.

But while God isn't a bully, some of the people who follow him sure are. For centuries we've seen people use God's name as a tool to bully those who are different from them. Even today, people picket, protest, and yell because they believe it's their God-given duty. Many Christians believe their calling here on earth is to pick apart the brokenness and failures of others, as if beating people down with their mess is the way to give them hope. But time and time again, I see this tactic fall short by miles. It does no good. In fact, it hurts.

This kind of mentality confuses me. It breaks my heart. And it's something that keeps me up at night. I struggle with the many pointed fingers that are used as weapons to speak shame instead of redemption, and I struggle with the extreme judgment that comes from most self-proclaimed cross bearers when someone in the public eye fails. Why do pastors and religious leaders choose to use the failures of others as sermon illustrations? Why do Christian bloggers spew personalized hatred toward someone for the sake of article shares and page views? Why do some churches bash other churches because "they're just not like us"? These are all questions I find myself pondering daily. God needs more champions of love and fewer religious trolls.

I sometimes wonder why God allows such examples of unlove to represent him. All of us fall short, but consistently living opposite of the way Jesus told us to is just outrageous. God must be shaking his head at the detrimental things being done in his name.

We can have different opinions, but our perspectives should be shared with love and sincerity, not with cruelty and rashness. Even when it's a matter of sin, we shouldn't let our responses become sinful in turn, misrepresenting the God we say we follow! It doesn't make sense to combat something we see as darkness with more darkness.

Yes, not all Christians have chosen to act this way—but a lot of people have. We can all make decisions out of our own sense of rightness that are actively unloving toward the people Jesus loves. When we do these things, our selfish ambitions cover up our love for God—and that isn't going to impress anyone into giving God a chance in his or her life.

It all comes back to a heart issue. When we act in unloving ways and portray God as the same, we are living out of sin and pride, which fuel us to think that it's our obligation to reprimand and rebuke others who are no better or worse than we are. This type of behavior doesn't help the expansion of God's love, nor does it help bring anyone to know the love of God. Fear isn't the way to convince people to have a relationship with God. The only way to do that is love. And remember, love is who God is.

Chapter 4

PRODIGAL LOVE

Getting baptized was probably one of the most memorable moments of my faith journey. Not only because my father baptized me but also because my younger brother was dunked underneath the water and raised to new life in Christ that day too. My baptism had been a long time coming. The old was gone, and the new had begun. I wish I could say this happened without any rebellious years, but that simply wasn't the case. I can't count how many times I've apologized to my father for the way I acted as a teenager. He always laughs and tells me that it's okay. But the reality is, it wasn't. I acted like a fool, I ignored my family, and I tried to find my way through life on my own. It wasn't until I came home to my heavenly Father that everything in my life changed, and I'm thankful that my earthly father welcomed me home with open arms as well. There were no questions, no comments, just open arms and compassion. I believe this type of love truly set me up for success in life. And this is the kind of love that we must be willing to show others, no matter how dark or desolate their state.

In Luke 15:11-32, Jesus paints the life-altering story of this kind of love—love for a son who continues to stray away from what's right, while all along his loving father waits for him at home.

> A man had two sons. The younger son told his father, "I want my share of your estate now before you die." So his father agreed to divide his wealth between his sons.
>
> LUKE 15:11-12

Asking for an early inheritance was outrageous. The younger son was essentially telling his father, "I wish you were already dead!" But the father accepted his son's wishes, even while knowing it probably wasn't the best idea. But one thing I've learned in life is that sometimes hearing wisdom from someone isn't enough.

I imagine this father and son saying their last good-byes, the father handing over the son's share of the inheritance and offering some final words of wisdom. "Make sure to put some of that money in savings," he may have said. "Don't spend it all in one place." But he knew his son was going to make his own decisions no matter what he said, and he had to take a step back and let it happen.

My father did exactly the same thing in a few situations. *He* saw the red flags, but my ignorance and immaturity blinded *me* from them. I was so excited about what was ahead of me that I ignored the nitty-gritty details and the possible obstacles. He knew the only way I'd learn was through trial and error, and sometimes that's the best way to show love to someone: giving that person all the wisdom you can up front, but allowing him or her to learn the hard way when your advice is ignored. Because you can't force someone to listen and accept what's right. That person has to do it of his or her own accord.

> A few days later this younger son packed all his belongings and moved to a distant land, and there he wasted all his money in wild living. About the time his money ran out, a great famine swept over the land, and he began to starve. He persuaded a local farmer to hire him, and the man sent him into his fields to feed the pigs. The young man became so hungry that even the pods he was feeding the pigs looked good to him. But no one gave him anything.
>
> LUKE 15:13-16

The younger son finds himself destitute and alone, as I imagine his father warned him about. The Bible says that "he wasted all his money in wild living," which we could guess included things such as gambling, prostitutes, luxurious living, and gluttony. The son lived like this until his money ran dry. I'm sure it all happened so fast in his mind. *Where did all my money go?* I imagine him thinking. And then . . . famine. Exactly when he needed his money the most, it was gone.

He was broke. He was alone. He was hungry. Trying to

persuade a local farmer to hire him was probably a lot harder than we think—the famine probably had everyone scraping to get by. But he managed to get a job feeding the pigs. And for someone who had nothing, that food started to look appetizing. Can you imagine going from living a lifestyle resembling that of royalty to feeding pigs and contemplating whether to join them because of how hungry you are? He went from the highest of highs to the lowest of lows in what probably seemed like the blink of an eye.

> When he finally came to his senses, he said to himself, "At home even the hired servants have food enough to spare, and here I am dying of hunger! I will go home to my father and say, 'Father, I have sinned against both heaven and you, and I am no longer worthy of being called your son. Please take me on as a hired servant.'"
> So he returned home to his father.
> LUKE 15:17-20

Something clicked within the son. His current circumstances in life were anything but where he wanted to be. And his heart began to change. The lifestyle he was living didn't satisfy his yearning for fulfillment. He was broken. And he came to his senses. His father's servants were better off than he was! They had a place to sleep, clean clothes, and bellies full of food—unlike him.

Eugene Peterson described the falsity of the world's lies like this: "The first step toward God is a step away from the lies of the world."[3] And that's what the son did. He decided it was time for him to drop his pride and head back home, probably wondering whether his father would even speak to him. *How on earth am I going to explain that my inheritance is gone?* he probably thought. But he had no other choice. He could either live with the pigs and pretend as if everything was okay or admit his failure and seek forgiveness from his father. And let's be honest—a lot of us sometimes would rather choose the first option than the second.

> While he was still a long way off, his father saw him coming. Filled with love and compassion, he ran to his son, embraced him, and kissed him. His son said to him, "Father, I have sinned against both heaven and you, and I am no longer worthy of being called your son."
>
> But his father said to the servants, "Quick! Bring the finest robe in the house and put it on him. Get a ring for his finger and sandals for his feet. And kill the calf we have been fattening. We must celebrate with a feast, for this son of mine was dead and has now returned to life. He was lost, but now he is found." So the party began.
>
> LUKE 15:20-24

I've read countless times that a man running toward another man in these times was not something you'd ordinarily see. Imagine how overwhelmed with emotion the father was when he saw his son in the distance. I would feel the same way seeing one of my kids in the distance. Verse 20 says, "Filled with love and compassion, he ran to his son, embraced him, and kissed him." I believe the father knew why his son was coming home. He knew that his money had been wasted. He knew that his son had done just what he had warned against—but still the father ran. And God still runs after us.

After the son admitted his failures, he probably expected his father to be upset and reprimand him, which would have been completely acceptable. But the father didn't do that. He did quite the opposite. The love that filled his heart led him to do something quite different. He welcomed his younger son with hugs, kisses, the finest robe in the house, sandals for his feet, and a gold ring for his finger. That's what love does. The father acts as if his son never left in the first place, welcoming him home with love, grace, and the best he has to offer.

A father's love for his children is something I never truly understood until I became a father myself. So I get it. I get why the father was so excited to see his boy returning home safe and in one piece. He couldn't contain his joy.

The son didn't expect any of this to happen—we know this because he said, "I am no longer worthy of being called your son" (verse 21). Convicted of his actions, he sought forgiveness from his father. And of course the father not only forgave him but also celebrated his return with a party and steak dinner.

> Meanwhile, the older son was in the fields working. When he returned home, he heard music and dancing in the house, and he asked one of the servants what was going on. "Your brother is back," he was told, "and your father has killed the fattened calf. We are celebrating because of his safe return."
>
> The older brother was angry and wouldn't go in. His father came out and begged him, but he replied, "All these years I've slaved for you and never once refused to do a single thing you told me to. And in all that time you never gave me even one young goat for a feast with my friends. Yet when this son of yours comes back after squandering your money on prostitutes, you celebrate by killing the fattened calf!"
>
> His father said to him, "Look, dear son, you have always stayed by me, and everything I have is yours. We had to celebrate this happy day. For your brother was dead and has come back to life! He was lost, but now he is found!"
>
> LUKE 15:25-32

The older brother wasn't too happy about the way his father responded. That's a heart issue. People who haven't truly encountered the love and grace of God don't know how to respond when others receive it. But they, too, are deeply loved. They, too, are called to come home.

This story is beautiful because both you and I are the Prodigal Son. The father is our Father in heaven, and the brother is those who have yet to truly experience the undeserved grace and compassion of God.

So much can be unpacked in this parable, but one of the richest truths is contained in one word: *prodigal.* How often do you hear that word outside of this story? It's not a word that frequently pops up in your Twitter feed, on TV, or in everyday conversation. Many of us, if pressed, probably couldn't define it. We often associate it with being lost and then returning. Its actual definition, however, is quite different. *Prodigal* has two common meanings:

1. "Spending money or resources freely and recklessly; wastefully extravagant."
2. "Having or giving something on a lavish scale."[4]

The first definition clearly applies to the younger son. He took his inheritance and spent it on lavish living, throwing years of his father's hard work and earnings down the drain. But the second definition also applies in this story—to the father. What happened when the son came home? Instead of chastising him for his reckless behavior, the father gave him a party on a lavish scale, killing the fattened calf and putting on a huge feast. That's prodigal love: love that is lavish and extravagant. Prodigal love is the love that Jesus has for us—so much more than what we deserve. No matter what we do, he just keeps pouring it out—covering us in his love—and he longs for our love in return. I meet a lot of people who say they wouldn't be caught dead inside a church building, that their lives are too messed up to be embraced by the arms of God, and that their previous failures are too monstrous to be forgiven by the grace of Jesus.

But no human is too broken for the all-consuming grace of our Lord and Savior. We've all done things we aren't proud of, said things that we wish we could take back, and been places we wouldn't dare go again. And while many of us have found redemption through the sacrifice of Jesus, we must remember that millions of other people in this world have yet to do the same.

The apostle Paul said in 1 Corinthians 15:9-10,

> For I am the least of all the apostles. In fact, I'm not even worthy to be called an apostle after the way I persecuted God's church.
>
> But whatever I am now, it is all because God poured out his special favor on me—and not without results. For I have worked harder than any of the other apostles; yet it was not I but God who was working through me by his grace.

The truth behind Paul's words is revitalizing and scandalous: that even a man who once persecuted the church of Jesus Christ has now been redeemed and forgiven by God's grace. A second chance awaited Paul through the transforming, prodigal love of Christ.

No matter what you've done, the grace and love of Jesus are waiting for you. You don't need to reach a certain level of "goodness" before you can pray, walk into a church, read a Bible, or even be used by God. He will take you where you are, but he loves you too much to leave you that way. Remember, nobody is too broken for the grace and love of Jesus.

God's love isn't only available to us when we're good. We're all prodigals in need of our Father's love. He's waiting for us with open arms when we decide to return home. And he'll even throw a party for us. That's how much he loves us.

Chapter 5

———————

L O V E   >   F E A R

Rick Warren once said that "fear is a self-imposed prison that will keep you from becoming what God intends for you to be. You *must* move against it with the weapons of faith and love."[5] And the most scared I've ever been in my life was on a roller coaster. I mean it! When I was serving as the next-gen pastor for a church, my wife and I led a trip to one of the biggest theme parks in the country. We took a total of three hundred teenagers, and I—the person who hates theme parks and roller coasters more than anything else in the world—had to chaperone the students on each and every ride. I assumed this would be the death of me.

Let me be really honest for a second. When I say I don't like roller coasters, I mean I *really* don't like roller coasters. I'm fine with sitting in a swing or in a log that gently slides into water or in colorful teacups that spin around. But a box that sits on a wooden or metal track and reaches speeds of more than fifty miles an hour? No, thanks. I'm done. (Don't even get me started on the ones where your feet dangle in the air like spaghetti noodles. I don't play those games.) I like my life, and I was created to walk on the ground. If I were supposed to fly at the speed of a small aircraft, God would have given me wings and a jetpack.

But . . . I couldn't let these kids who I was technically pastoring think I was a total loser for not joining them on the rides. Did I mention that this was my first week as their pastor? I couldn't be the guy who just waited for them at the exit. Nobody would respect that guy. I had to face my fears head-on and pray that God would keep me from screaming like a little kid in front of the teens to whom I had literally just preached a message about having faith in the midst of fears. (I'm sure God was laughing at me.)

The first few rides the kids chose were a piece of cake. Nothing I couldn't handle. Maybe I would actually get lucky and make it through the day without having to face my fears. But just as I assumed I was in the clear, I heard a student say five terrifying words: "Let's go on that one." He was pointing to something that looked as high as the sun. The teens screamed in excitement, while my heart rate began to speed up and my palms began to sweat. As I watched, a group of people on the ride passed by us, their feet dangling and flailing around as they hit loop after loop.

My wife gave me a smile that said, *Ha!* She knew I had no way of getting out of this one. "Okay," I said. "Let's do it!"

The next twenty minutes in line were the longest twenty minutes of my life. Fear had taken over. I was a little shaky in the knees, which wasn't helped by the Coca-Cola I downed every time the line stopped moving. (I was stress drinking.

Don't judge.) The thunderous sound of the coaster echoed through the theme park, and the screams of grown men and women were painful to my ears.

We finally made our way to the front of the line. When people who went before us stepped out of their seats, the world seemed to stop. It was just me and that stupid roller coaster, facing off against each other. Just imagine the Israelites shuddering as Goliath taunted them from the other side of the valley. (I wasn't Goliath.) I had to muster up every ounce of courage I had just to take a step forward and buckle myself into that death trap.

Silly as it may sound, I prayed to God that I'd be safe. I'd heard crazy stories about roller coasters coming off their tracks, and I didn't want to be one of those rare statistics. But if I was going to die on this roller coaster, at least I knew where I'd end up. So that gave me a little comfort. Desperate times call for desperate measures, my friends. I was conquering one of my biggest fears. And whatever we may face, no matter how silly the fear may seem, the love of God meets us in our time of need. Because the reality is, sometimes life feels a lot like a roller coaster.

We shot off at what seemed like the speed of a small rocket, made a quick left turn, and then went straight up into a loop. I gripped the shoulder straps as hard as I could and tried to make sure I took normal breaths so I didn't pass out. As we hit the second loop and began to fly over the theme park, something within me changed. My screams of fear slowly turned into screams of excitement. When we got to one of the highest points of the ride, I could see for miles and miles. The view was beautiful. And I wouldn't have been able to see it if I had let my fear get in the way. All these years I had been afraid of roller coasters, but I had never actually taken the opportunity to experience one.

I believe our fears and roller coasters have a lot in common, particularly when God's love is part of it. What starts as ups, downs, and uncertainty is quickly overcome by excitement, contentment, and joy. Why? Because when we step out in faith, our fear is gone. Having the courage to lean into the fear helps us conquer it. When God's perfect love is part of our lives, our fears have no place to reside and we can enjoy the beautiful view. The Bible doesn't say that fear won't ever exist, but it does say that it has no place in telling us how we should live. Fear is no match for God's perfect love. Fear is no match for God.

Perfect Love

What's keeping you from being brave? What's keeping you from chasing your dreams and becoming the person God has called you to be?

My insecurities and doubts constantly distract me from the truth that God gives me. But again and again I'm reminded that the Bible tells us that perfect love casts out all fear: the fear of the unknown and the fear of what lies ahead. As we learn to embrace the love of God, we gain the courage to step out in faith and embrace the wondrous journey of the Christian life. This might sound easier said than done. But I believe that with practice and experience, we can all come to the realization that stepping out in faith toward the will of God always brings us closer to him—and closer to conquering our fears.

Maybe you have a fear of relationships, of failure, of the opinions of others, of starting your own company, of getting married, of having kids, of traveling to the other side of the world. Maybe you fear something that doesn't feel rational, such as heights, spiders, or the dark. Maybe you've gone through something traumatic, and paralyzing fear has a grip on your life. Our fears occupy a vast spectrum, from silly to serious, mild to severe, temporary to long-term.

It's a good thing we don't have to let fear control the way we live our lives.

Yep, you read that right. Your fear doesn't have to define you. It doesn't have to be permanent. It doesn't have to control you. It doesn't even have a right to exist in your life when Jesus is there with you. Now, I'm not saying I have it all figured out—trust me, I'm still working through my own fears, just as you are. The fear of what others think about me, the fear of failure, and the fear of not being good enough. But each and every moment I spend with God, a small piece of those fears is chipped away.

In 1 John 4:18, we learn that "there is no fear in love. But perfect love drives out fear, because fear has to do with punishment. The one who fears is not made perfect in love" (NIV). All things can be conquered with the love of God. How do we know this? Because the beautiful words of Scripture state it to be true. It's that simple. When we go through life in the power of the love of God, discomfort, fear, and opposition will be matched with God's power and favor. This love is a conqueror, and it will fight for you.

He's Already Been There

Fear can paralyze even the bravest and strongest of individuals. Fear causes you to sometimes doubt yourself and the opportunities that may come your way, to second-guess your capabilities, and to fall silent when you know that you should be speaking up. We all deal with fear, but the way we respond to it can drastically change how it affects us.

Alexander Maclaren said this about the fear John wrote about in 1 John 4:18:

> John has been speaking of boldness, and that
> naturally suggests its opposite—fear. . . . Perfect love
> produces courage in the day of judgment, because
> it produces likeness to Christ, who is the Judge. In
> my text he explains and enlarges that statement.
> For there is another way in which love produces
> boldness, and that is by its casting out fear. These

two are mutually exclusive. The entrance of the one
is for the other a notice to quit. We cannot both love
and fear the same person or thing, and where love
comes in, the darker form slips out at the door; and
where Love comes in, it brings hand in hand with
itself Courage with her radiant face. But boldness
is the companion of love, only when love is perfect.
For, inconsistent as the two emotions are, love, in its
earlier stages and lower degrees, is often perturbed
and dashed by apprehension and dread.

Now John is speaking about the two emotions
in themselves, irrespective, so far as his language
goes, of the objects to which they are directed. What
he is saying is true about love and fear, whatever
or whosoever may be loved or dreaded. But the
context suggests the application in his mind, for it
is "boldness before him" about which he has been
speaking; and so it is love and fear directed towards
God which are meant in my text. The experience
of hosts of professing Christians is only too forcible
a comment upon the possibility of a partial Love
lodging in the heart side by side with a fellow-lodger,
Fear, whom it ought to have expelled.[6]

Time and time again in the Bible, we see people facing fear
that wants to keep them from pursuing what God has called
them to: Joshua battling the Amorites (see Joshua 10:12),

Moses looking out over the Red Sea (see Exodus 14:21), and Noah being told to build the ark (see Genesis 5–10). These individuals could have let fear overcome them, but their love for God pushed them to trust. And God in turn took care of them in the face of fear. The sun stood still; the waters parted; Noah's family was saved. God was there, guiding them every step of the way, even if the steps weren't made clear in the moment. We fear because we're human, but we choose to dwell in God's love because we are his children.

We must understand that God's support and assistance in the face of fear are still available and true today. God isn't just watching you or standing next to you in this journey called life—he's leading the front lines.

"Do not be afraid or discouraged," Deuteronomy 31:8 tells us, "for the LORD will personally go ahead of you. He will be with you; he will neither fail you nor abandon you." This powerful truth is both assuring and comforting: God will go ahead of us, God will be with us, God will not abandon us. We have no need to worry about the present or future because God, who is outside of time itself, has already been where we are going. He's all-powerful, all-knowing, and all-forgiving. God knows what will take place in our lives, and we can rely on his love in times of fear and trouble.

When we put our lives in God's hands, we can rest, knowing that he has everything under his control. Now, this doesn't mean that fear will be absent from our thoughts or that we are no longer allowed to fear. Rather, fear no longer needs to control the way we live, dream, speak, and act, because fear sits under the colossal majesty of God.

Sarah's Story

When I think about love conquering fear, I'm reminded of a girl named Sarah.

I used to be the manager of a small Christian bookstore in Orange County, California. The store was unlike any other retail space I've seen since; it bridged the gap between faith and culture in such a beautiful way. People from all different walks of life came through its doors—ex-convicts, pastors, teenagers, tourists, college students, missionaries, political leaders, gay and lesbian couples, grandparents, professional athletes, military service members, drug addicts. You'd be surprised by how many people with no religious background would find their way inside the store, simply out of curiosity. Well . . . I'd call it the Holy Spirit.

Some people were looking for books, others for clothing or music. We had everything, and all of it pointed back to our faith in God. We were encouraged to pray with every customer who walked through our doors, and we were even directed to lead people to Christ if they wanted to know more, regardless of what the register lines looked like. That little store helped truly shape my relationship with God and the way I view what it means to be the church. I learned how to manage people, talk to people, and listen to people in a way I had never experienced before. Some of the employees are now worship leaders, full-time missionaries, or even pastors. The culture of that store helped all of us understand how to work hard and exude a life of love regardless of where we ended up.

It was at this little store that I met Sarah. One Friday night near closing time, just as one of the employees and I were about to close the gate and begin counting out our registers, I saw a young girl and a woman who I assumed was her mom staring inside the store, looking excited. I'd be lying if I said I wanted them to come in. I was tired and ready to head home for the night. Boy, am I glad that God contradicted my expectations.

"This store is amazing!" Sarah said, laughing. "California has so much Jesus in it!"

"How can I help you today?" I asked them. Both began to explain how excited they were to see a store like this in a mall, and Sarah told me how much she loved attending youth group while visiting her aunt for the month. A little confused, I asked Sarah where she was from.

She began to explain that she was visiting her aunt in California while stuff at home settled down a bit. When I asked her to explain what she meant, the floodgates opened. Her eyes started to well up, and her shoulders sank. Her aunt then stepped in. "Sarah hasn't had the best high school experience," she said.

Sarah's aunt explained that Sarah's family lives in a small

JARRID WILSON

town of about four hundred people in the Midwest. Her family is one of only a few Christian families in their town, and because of her faith, Sarah has been picked on at school more times than she'd like to admit. Someone spray-painted "666" on the side of Sarah's house; many times when she was praying over her lunch, girls threw gum in her hair; and she had even been stabbed with a pencil in the locker room.

This was just a small fraction of the bullying she had experienced over the years. When Sarah's family tried to address the situation with her teachers and the local author-ities, they got a response that nobody would have expected: "If you don't like living here, then leave. We can't prove that anything you said is true. They're just kids."

As Sarah and her aunt told me this story, I was speech-less. My eyes were opened to the harsh reality of what some people face, even in the United States, for their faith in Jesus. I mean, we hear about persecution all around the world, but rarely do we hear of physical attacks against Christians in this country.

As I listened to Sarah's story, part of me was sad, while another part of me was angry. I wanted nothing more than to pick up all my things and go teach some high school kids a lesson, though that would probably not have been the smartest of decisions. *Maybe you could move in with your aunt and live here in California.* But when I suggested this to Sarah and her aunt, they both shook their heads. I've held Sarah's response close to my heart ever since. She wiped away the tears from her eyes, looked at me with assurance, and said, "I can't leave because I believe God has me there to change my town."

Silence.

I could not believe the words that had just come out of this fourteen-year-old's mouth. She said it with such confidence—a God-fearing boldness that I could hear in her voice. It took me by surprise, and it was the last thing I had expected her to say. It reminded me of something Eugene Peterson wrote:

> The only opportunity you will ever have to live by faith is in the circumstances you are provided this very day: this house you live in, this family you find yourself in, this job you have been given, the weather conditions that prevail at this moment.[7]

We have opportunities each and every day to live out the love of God, even when fear might push us to do otherwise. Sometimes that just means staying where we are and radically loving those who are around us. Sarah had every reason to leave her small town, but that also gave her even more of a reason to stay. Loving in the face of fear sometimes means staying when it's easier to leave, relying on Christ to keep you grounded and secure.

I think we can learn a lot from my friend Sarah. Despite living in a situation in which most people would be afraid for their safety, she continues to put God first, allowing his love to fuel her and also longing to see her minuscule town be changed by Jesus.

Would I have had the same courage if I had been Sarah? Courageously loving God and loving others despite fear and persecution is what it looks like to truly live for God. That's true faith. That's what it means to be a devoted disciple of Jesus. If Christians were to stop pursuing the love of God every time fear came into the picture, we'd get nowhere. Fear must be met face-to-face, all in the name of Jesus. Because true love is always going to overcome fear.

Chapter 6

———————

GOD *and the* GARBAGE DUMP

Over the last few years of my life, I've spent quite a bit of time outside the country, speaking, hosting events, and writing through my experiences with different organizations. But a recent trip to Nicaragua completely changed my perspective on what it means for God's love to transcend the circumstances of our lives.

When I was invited by a nonprofit here in the United States to go on a trip to Nicaragua, I quickly cleared my schedule and prepared myself for the adventure that I knew was to come. I've always loved visiting new places, and my wife and I have made it a point to never turn down new experiences in new settings, regardless of how out of place we might feel. On this trip to Nicaragua, I'd be spending almost two weeks visiting orphanages, working on service projects, and learning more about the needs of the country.

After our plane landed, our group of about twelve was escorted through customs, and then we gathered our things and made our way to a few small vans that were waiting for us. We were from all different walks of life: pastors, authors, bloggers, conference overseers, and even business owners.

And we all had one thing in common: a heart for people in need and a vibrant love for God.

After we were dropped off at our hotel, we all sat down for dinner, a traditional Nicaraguan meal of some type of wonderful meat and beans, and Coca-Cola in glass bottles. We learned whom we'd be sharing rooms with and we got to know one another as we laughed, joked, and bantered back and forth about our lives and ministry back home. It was a beautiful communal experience that none of us seemed to want to end. But while we sat comfortably in our chairs and filled our bellies with the best of Nicaraguan cuisine, we were warned that the next day was not going to be easy. There would be no gentle easing into the brokenness that existed in this country, and it was going to be an experience we would never forget.

I called my wife, Juli, to see how the family was doing, fill her in about all that had happened since our arrival and the people I had met, and ask her to pray for our team. When I travel out of the country, I normally don't switch over my phone plan to work out of network and instead rely on free Wi-Fi for communication and connectivity. There's something beautiful about unplugging and finding the freedom to experience what God has planned. When I don't have the luxury of posting, texting, and e-mailing, I'm forced to keep my heart focused on what's in front of me.

Juli prayed for me over the phone, and at about the same time, my roommate's wife was doing the same for him. I still remember how oddly and beautifully timed that was. Juli prayed for security, for boldness, and that God might use me however he saw fit. She prayed that my heart would not worry about anything, that I would trust in God for what he had planned for me, and that I would come home with more understanding and knowledge than ever before. It was a mighty and audacious prayer.

After hanging up, I spent some time chatting with my roommate, Matt, then prayed and read some of my Bible before heading to bed. I felt as if God had something big he wanted to show me the next day—as though he was telling me that something great was going to happen. I sensed that God was going to blow my expectations out of the water. I went to sleep that night with my heart fixed in a posture of learning.

The next morning I was filled with excitement and hesitation as I wondered how the day was going to pan out. After we all gathered in the hotel lobby, we were given schedules that would keep us on track, as well as phone numbers in case any of us got disconnected from the group. (I'm pretty sure those numbers were specifically for me. I tend to wander.) My friend Brad welcomed all of us, thanked us for being part of the trip, and explained how excited he was for us to see the incredible work that was taking place within the organization. We gathered closer together and prayed that God would work in miraculous ways, that our hearts would be opened, and that our time in Nicaragua would not be without merit. We ended with a big "Amen" and made our way to the convoy of buses.

As the bus I was in bounced over the potholed roads, I stared out the window and tried to take in as much as I could. I forced myself to notice the faces of people we passed, the restaurants that looked as though they were about to cave in on themselves, and the plethora of livestock that roamed the streets during the early mornings. I took pictures so that I could capture the moments that I knew were already having an impact on my life. The farther we drove, the worse the surrounding areas became. While Nicaragua was quite beautiful, these areas we were traveling through were clearly hurting.

In one place, it seemed as though a bomb had exploded and everyone was living within the rubble. Whole families stood outside the makeshift doorways, leaning on the bricks that remained solid, and they smiled and waved to us as we passed by. The hardships these people were facing put a lot into perspective for me. Things I hadn't really ever thought about until now. To think that only a few days prior, I was complaining about the speed of my Internet or that my coffee tasted a little burned. Even before we reached our first destination, I was tearing up. I quickly wiped my eyes, looked over to my friend Brad, and said, "Thank you for inviting me on this trip." He didn't have to say anything. He knew what I was feeling. He smiled and patted me on the back as if to say, "You're welcome."

Before I had any time to gather myself, the smell of rotten trash and smoke started to permeate the ventilation system of our bus. I was confused. We were on a stretch of man-made road *in the middle of a garbage dump*. Trash, trash, and more trash as far as the eye could see. We had arrived in a place I had only heard about: La Chureca, the largest open-air landfill in Central America.

As I quickly tried to cover my nose, I caught a glimpse of something moving among the garbage. I assumed it was a street dog or even a bird, but I was wrong.

One, then two, and then three little girls climbed out of the garbage heap, holding small pitchforks and wearing what appeared to be homemade masks to dampen the smell and filter the smoke. Our guides explained that the children were searching the dump for food and small items to sell. The pitchforks helped them avoid using their hands to dig through the rubble and possibly getting cut by sharp objects. Each girl had wood on the bottoms of her shoes to keep nails from piercing through the rubber. *This can't be real*, I thought. I broke down as I realized what these little children had to go through each and every day.

But then I noticed something I'll never forget.

They were smiling. Genuine joy. Gratefulness. Happiness.

When we stepped off the bus, nearly one hundred people emerged from the piles of garbage around us. As they greeted us and then lined up, we learned why we were here: We were to feed these men, women, and children who had to dig through the trash of this dump to find a way to provide for themselves.

I was told I could venture away from the group and spend some time walking around with three children as they dug for and scooped up specific items from the garbage: clothing, electronics, scrap metal—anything that could be sold to help provide for their families. These children were searching for things that I throw away. Items that I considered no longer useful were their means of provision.

One little girl had big eyes and a smile that could light up any room. Feeling the sun beating down on us, I took off my bandanna and placed it on her head to keep it from being scorched. She nodded as if to say thank you. I knelt down and asked her, "*¿Cómo te llamas?*" ("What is your name?") She paused for a second and giggled with her friends, then gave me a big smile and said, "*Me llamo Julie. ¿Y tú?*" ("My name is Julie. And you?")

Really, God? Her name is Julie? I couldn't hold back my tears. "*Me llamo Jarrid,*" I said to this beautiful, joy-filled little girl who shared my wife's name. The people around me probably thought I was crazy, but I was so overwhelmed already—and now this? I couldn't hold back the emotion. When she pointed at the regrettably massive cross tattoo on my chest and then put her hands over her heart, smiled, and said, "Jesus!" I had to laugh. It felt as though God was speaking to me in a deep and profound way, right here in a garbage dump in the heart of Nicaragua.

I made my way back to the line of families who were waiting to obtain their bags of rice and beans, and I asked our translators how many people here knew about God or had any type of religious beliefs. He told me that many of the people were in fact part of small Christian churches in the area and that we'd later see one while visiting the orphanage and school. Some of the men even volunteered in pastoral roles, he said.

Suddenly something clicked into place. The people around me had nothing in terms of wealth or success—nothing we'd typically use to explain the aroma of joy and hope surrounding them. And yes, I was getting only a glimpse of their experience—a glimpse of the very hard realities they faced, the struggle to simply survive. But even that glimpse, even the briefest sense of the joy they lived out of despite their circumstances, reminded me of what the true source of our joy should always be: the love of God. As we embrace and live out of his love, a spirit of fulfillment brings us to a place of peace, no matter what we're facing.

These people had nothing. But in reality, they had everything—just as you and I do, with or without any of our material successes. In the love of God, we have everything we need. I wish my joy for Christ in every circumstance was more like Julie's. Later on that day, as I saw her worshiping God with lifted hands and pure joy, I sensed her fulfillment and security in knowing she was his child.

What would our lives look like if we found our purpose in the love of God and not in material things or circumstances?

What lives we could truly live. What contentment we could truly find! So often we seek God's love because we think he'll then gift us with the lives we want, but the reality is that God's love is the gift. That's the prize. His love is everything our hearts and souls desire. He is what we need to weather the storms of life. The love of God transcends circumstances.

We tend to forget this in the United States. We search after worth and identity in all the wrong places: how many followers we have on social media, what kind of cars we have, the size of our houses. So many of us complain about what we don't have, but generally, our lives are pretty comfortable. In fact, millions of people around the world are praying for the very things we take for granted—food, shelter, health care, the basic necessities of life. Many of us have rooms for our cars to live in, while others around the world are scavenging for reliable shelter. Materially, we may have it better—but do we really? Comfort makes it easy to rely on our possessions and circumstances rather than rest in the love of God. Maybe this is why Jesus said in Matthew, "Blessed are the poor in spirit, for theirs is the kingdom of heaven" (5:3, NIV).

Finding contentment and worth in God's love is a daily fight and a daily choice. But even when that foundation is shaken, God is always there, waiting for us to turn back to him. People who have nothing or face persecution or are struggling with chronic illness sometimes seem to find it easier to rest in God's love, because it's easier to rest in his love when everything else is stripped away. When we have nothing else to hold on to, the gospel of Jesus transforms the way we see life. In this place, we truly get what it means to rely on God for everything in life.

Every. Little. Thing.

Whether you have hot meals delivered to your house or you're rummaging through a garbage dump for scraps, God's love is the only thing that can bring joy and peace and fulfillment to your life. Elisabeth Elliot said it best:

> Where does your security lie? Is God your refuge, your hiding place, your stronghold, your shepherd, your counselor, your friend, your redeemer, your saviour, your guide? If He is, you don't need to search any further for security.[8]

Chapter 7

UNSHAKEN

No matter who we are or what we're facing, we can find unshakable rest and security in the love of God. We see the proof of this all throughout Scripture! Take Paul and Silas. Their faith in the midst of trials shows us just what it looks like to place our hope and confidence in who God is, not in who we are or what we have or what we have done.

In Acts 16:16-35, we read about Paul and Silas being thrown into prison for healing a demon-possessed girl.

> One day as we were going down to the place of prayer, we met a slave girl who had a spirit that enabled her to tell the future. She earned a lot of money for her masters by telling fortunes. She followed Paul and the rest of us, shouting, "These men are servants of the Most High God, and they have come to tell you how to be saved."
>
> This went on day after day until Paul got so exasperated that he turned and said to the demon within her, "I command you in the name of Jesus Christ to come out of her." And instantly it left her.

Her masters' hopes of wealth were now shattered, so they grabbed Paul and Silas and dragged them before the authorities at the marketplace. "The whole city is in an uproar because of these Jews!" they shouted to the city officials. "They are teaching customs that are illegal for us Romans to practice."

A mob quickly formed against Paul and Silas, and the city officials ordered them stripped and beaten with wooden rods. They were severely beaten, and then they were thrown into prison. The jailer was ordered to make sure they didn't escape. So the jailer put them into the inner dungeon and clamped their feet in the stocks.

ACTS 16:16-24

The demonic possession had made the girl profitable for her masters, so when Paul cast the demon out, her owners weren't pleased, to say the least. They dragged both men to face the authorities in the marketplace, claiming Paul and Silas were breaking the law. They were stripped, beaten, flogged, and placed in an inner cell with stocks fastened around their feet.

In the midst of this horrific experience, something amazing happened: Paul and Silas began to praise God from the depths of their prison cell. When their circumstances became unbearable, they could have complained. But instead they turned to the only one who is constant no matter our circumstances. It was either complete insanity—or God's rich love dwelling within their hearts.

> Around midnight Paul and Silas were praying and singing hymns to God, and the other prisoners were listening.
> ACTS 16:25

Note that God didn't stop them from being arrested, didn't stop them from being beaten, didn't keep them from prison just because they were his followers. When we're in the midst of storms, he doesn't promise that he'll take us out of them. But he does promise that we won't be swept away.

And so Paul and Silas worshiped and praised with no expectation that God would take them out of that cell.

Yet God did just that.

> Suddenly, there was a massive earthquake, and the prison was shaken to its foundations. All the doors immediately flew open, and the chains of every prisoner fell off! The jailer woke up to see the prison doors wide open. He assumed the prisoners had escaped, so he drew his sword to kill himself. But Paul shouted to him, "Stop! Don't kill yourself! We are all here!"
>
> The jailer called for lights and ran to the dungeon and fell down trembling before Paul and

Silas. Then he brought them out and asked, "Sirs, what must I do to be saved?"

They replied, "Believe in the Lord Jesus and you will be saved, along with everyone in your household." And they shared the word of the Lord with him and with all who lived in his household. Even at that hour of the night, the jailer cared for them and washed their wounds. Then he and everyone in his household were immediately baptized. He brought them into his house and set a meal before them, and he and his entire household rejoiced because they all believed in God.

The next morning the city officials sent the police to tell the jailer, "Let those men go!"

ACTS 16:26-35

The God who allowed them to be thrown into a prison cell is the same God who didn't allow them to be kept captive for long. He sent an earthquake that not only freed them from their shackles but also destroyed the prison walls around them. And God's plan didn't end with their freedom. He reached out in love to their captor—in fact, his love for the jailer may have been the very reason Paul and Silas were sent to that cell. That man, along with his entire household, chose to follow Christ. A complete heart transformation— all because two men placed their security in the love of God and not in their circumstances. Nothing could shake the foundation, which itself shook the very foundation of that prison.

We see something similar happen in chapter 3 of the book of Daniel.

> King Nebuchadnezzar made a gold statue ninety feet tall and nine feet wide and set it up on the plain of Dura in the province of Babylon. Then he sent messages to the high officers, officials, governors, advisers, treasurers, judges, magistrates, and all the provincial officials to come to the dedication of the statue he had set up. So all these officials came and stood before the statue King Nebuchadnezzar had set up.
>
> Then a herald shouted out, "People of all races and nations and languages, listen to the king's command! When you hear the sound of the horn, flute, zither, lyre, harp, pipes, and other musical instruments, bow to the ground to worship King Nebuchadnezzar's gold statue. Anyone who refuses to obey will immediately be thrown into a blazing furnace."
>
> So at the sound of the musical instruments, all the people, whatever their race or nation or language, bowed to the ground and worshiped the gold statue that King Nebuchadnezzar had set up.
>
> DANIEL 3:1-7

Three men—Shadrach, Meshach, and Abednego—had been taken captive and put in the service of King Nebuchadnezzar, who was busy directing the construction of this ninety-foot-tall and nine-foot-wide gold statue of himself for all his people to worship and bow down to. And, as we read, if anyone refused to worship it, he or she would be thrown into a blazing furnace. (A tip to anyone whose leader demands you worship a golden statue: Don't listen. That person is crazy.)

But Shadrach, Meshach, and Abednego were all for the mission of God despite being captives and despite being put in a situation in which their lives were at risk.

> Some of the astrologers went to the king and informed on the Jews. They said to King Nebuchadnezzar, "Long live the king! You issued a decree requiring all the people to bow down and worship the gold statue when they hear the sound of the horn, flute, zither, lyre, harp, pipes, and other musical instruments. That decree also states that those who refuse to obey must be thrown into a blazing furnace. But there are some Jews—Shadrach, Meshach, and Abednego—whom you have put in charge of the province of Babylon. They pay no attention to you, Your Majesty. They refuse to serve your gods and do not worship the gold statue you have set up."
>
> DANIEL 3:8-12

These three men weren't about to worship any god other than the one true God. And they were determined to trust the power of God in the midst of a situation most of us would try to do anything to get ourselves out of.

When Nebuchadnezzar heard that these three men were refusing to worship his statue, he wasn't too happy.

> Then Nebuchadnezzar flew into a rage and ordered that Shadrach, Meshach, and Abednego be brought before him. When they were brought in, Nebuchadnezzar said to them, "Is it true, Shadrach, Meshach, and Abednego, that you refuse to serve my gods or to worship the gold statue I have set up? I will give you one more chance to bow down and worship the statue I have made when you hear the sound of the musical instruments. But if you refuse, you will be thrown immediately into the blazing furnace. And then what god will be able to rescue you from my power?"
>
> Shadrach, Meshach, and Abednego replied, "O Nebuchadnezzar, we do not need to defend ourselves before you. If we are thrown into the blazing furnace, the God whom we serve is able to save us. He will rescue us from your power, Your Majesty. But even if he doesn't, we want to make it clear to you, Your Majesty, that we will never serve your gods or worship the gold statue you have set up."
>
> DANIEL 3:13-18

I assume Nebuchadnezzar was expecting them to change their minds after he threatened them a bit, but that's definitely not what happened. All three of the men likely knew the outcome of their refusal wasn't going to be great, but they continued to trust that following the God who loved them was worth any cost.

I find myself marveling at the boldness and faithfulness of these men. They were so consumed and secure in their love for God that they were willing to risk it all. They weren't shaken by the situation. They believed that following God mattered so much more than the approval of man. That's what truly allowing the love of God to infiltrate your life looks like. You can live with the certainty, security, and boldness that, no matter your circumstances, choosing to follow God is always the right choice.

As you might expect, Nebuchadnezzar wasn't particularly happy with the answer he got from the three men. He did as promised: He threw Shadrach, Meshach, and Abednego into the blazing furnace.

> Nebuchadnezzar was so furious with Shadrach, Meshach, and Abednego that his face became distorted with rage. He commanded that the furnace be heated seven times hotter than usual. Then he ordered some of the strongest men of his army to bind Shadrach, Meshach, and Abednego and throw them into the blazing furnace. So they tied them

up and threw them into the furnace, fully dressed in their pants, turbans, robes, and other garments. And because the king, in his anger, had demanded such a hot fire in the furnace, the flames killed the soldiers as they threw the three men in. So Shadrach, Meshach, and Abednego, securely tied, fell into the roaring flames.

DANIEL 3:19-23

Now, many of us know this story well. But as I read it again, I saw it in a new way—through the lens of God's love.

God's love for the men didn't mean that he stopped them from being thrown into the fire. Just as with Paul and Silas, and just as in our own lives, God loving us doesn't mean we aren't going to face impossible circumstances. Rather, God's love means that we can enter those situations with the confidence that we are loved—the confidence that our foundation is secure. God might not protect us from experiencing trials in our lives, but he gives us everything we need to persevere and cling more closely to him. God might not protect us from experiencing brokenness in our lives, but his love offers a means of deep and unexpected healing.

Of course, just as God intervened powerfully with Paul and Silas, he stepped in and saved Shadrach, Meshach, and Abednego. And when the three men emerged from the furnace unharmed, protected by God's power, they didn't even smell like smoke.

Suddenly, Nebuchadnezzar jumped up in amazement and exclaimed to his advisers, "Didn't we tie up three men and throw them into the furnace?"

"Yes, Your Majesty, we certainly did," they replied.

"Look!" Nebuchadnezzar shouted. "I see four men, unbound, walking around in the fire unharmed! And the fourth looks like a god!"

Then Nebuchadnezzar came as close as he could to the door of the flaming furnace and shouted: "Shadrach, Meshach, and Abednego, servants of the Most High God, come out! Come here!"

So Shadrach, Meshach, and Abednego stepped out of the fire. Then the high officers, officials, governors, and advisers crowded around them and saw that the fire had not touched them. Not a hair on their heads was singed, and their clothing was not scorched. They didn't even smell of smoke!

DANIEL 3:24-27

Once again, God's love extends beyond saving us from our present circumstances. His goal is always to speak of that love to us and to those who don't know him. Nebuchadnezzar was front and center to God's work. He had no choice but to acknowledge the incredible power of this God of Shadrach, Meshach, and Abednego.

> Nebuchadnezzar said, "Praise to the God of
> Shadrach, Meshach, and Abednego! He sent his
> angel to rescue his servants who trusted in him.
> They defied the king's command and were willing
> to die rather than serve or worship any god except
> their own God. Therefore, I make this decree: If any
> people, whatever their race or nation or language,
> speak a word against the God of Shadrach, Meshach,
> and Abednego, they will be torn limb from limb,
> and their houses will be turned into heaps of rubble.
> There is no other god who can rescue like this!"
>
> DANIEL 3:28-29

These stories of God working on behalf of those he loves, even and especially in the midst of impossibly hard circumstances, remind me of Isaiah 43:2:

> When you go through deep waters,
>   I will be with you.
> When you go through rivers of difficulty,
>   you will not drown.
> When you walk through the fire of oppression,
>   you will not be burned up;
>   the flames will not consume you.

God doesn't always save us from physical harm. His love doesn't mean our circumstances always change in the way we want them to. But his love *does* mean that he never leaves us. It means that we are never alone and that he is working for a greater story than we can ever imagine. Trusting that love is the only path to true peace in life.

When we rely on God, his love, and his promises—when we let God's love fuel our souls—he will bring us through whatever we're walking through. Just keep singing. Just keep praising God. Just keep living in his love. Don't let the world entice you with the many other so-called fulfillments that it has to offer. None of them can stand the test of time or bear all that life has to offer.

We all look to many different sources of contentment, but nothing except the love of God will hold fast when the winds and waves of life come crashing down on top of us. The love of God is deeper and more satisfying than anything we can imagine. It's the oxygen that keeps us alive, the very roots that keep us grounded, and our unshakable foundation.

The Tale of Two Houses

When I was about sixteen years old, a massive storm descended on the Gulf Coast. Rarely did the West Coast, where I lived, experience this kind of life-threatening weather, so my family and I were intrigued as to what was taking place. The storm had everyone scared and running inland for protection, while the rest of the country watched in horror and prayed for the safety of those being affected. My family huddled around the television and watched the hurricane bring its worst, while people on the Gulf Coast took shelter where they could.

The winds were too powerful for helicopters to take flight, so the brave newscasters risked their lives on the ground to broadcast the craziness of the storm.

Because we were in Southern California, we really had nothing to stress about, but we were worried for the people who remained in the midst of the storm and had yet to make their way to safety. People live in houses of all shapes and sizes along the Gulf Coast—tall and short, wide and narrow, mansions and shacks. Some people have lived there in the same houses for decades, while others have demolished old ones to build something new on their dream spots of land. But storms don't care what kind of house you live in. They have only one job: to be a storm.

Our family watched as the waves got bigger, the winds grew stronger, and the debris that was being tossed around became larger. We could hear the fear in the news anchor's voice as the camera turned toward two houses. One appeared to be a beautiful newly built home—the kind with six bedrooms, a beautiful pool, a rooftop balcony, and probably its own theater room. The other house looked as though it were out of an old surfer movie—a shack that had clearly been built decades before. Both were at the mercy of the crashing waves.

"The waves are getting higher!" the news anchor said as he sought refuge in a parking garage. "I hope the owners of these homes have evacuated." And at that moment, the camera captured a wave—then another and another—crashing on top of the houses. And then finally a massive tide of water covered every inch of both houses. You could have heard a pin drop in my family's living room. We prayed that nobody was stuck inside those homes.

When the water began descending, we saw something no one expected. The newly built home was destroyed—unrecognizable, turned to rubble—and the little shack remained sturdy and strong. It was exactly the opposite of what you would have thought. Then the news anchor made a statement that I'll never forget. He looked into the camera in disbelief and said, "Wow! They just don't make them like they used to."

His statement shook me to the core. It reminded me of Jesus' words in Matthew 7:24-27 (ESV):

> Everyone then who hears these words of mine and does them will be like a wise man who built his house on the rock. And the rain fell, and the floods came, and the winds blew and beat on that house, but it did not fall, because it had been founded on the rock. And everyone who hears these words of mine and does not do them will be like a foolish man who built his house on the sand. And the rain fell, and the floods came, and the winds blew and beat against that house, and it fell, and great was the fall of it.

According to Jesus, we can choose either to build our houses (our faith) on the rock—Jesus—or else to build our houses on the sand—the world. Both are foundations, but only one will last. Only one of them will withstand the storms we face. Only placing our faith in Jesus will bring us closer to him and help us live out of his best for us: his will.

Now, I don't believe that the mansion on the coast was actually built on sand, but I think the comparison makes sense. Think about the reporter's words: "They just don't make them like they used to." Houses today often aren't made with as much diligence as those built one hundred, fifty, or even twenty-five years ago. We live in a culture that wants to get things done as quickly as possible, sometimes skipping over small but crucial details. And although that little beach shack probably cost a fraction of what the mansion did, its foundation was strong, likely the result of careful planning and building. We should build our lives with God in the same way. You can't rush true love, and building a relationship with God is a marathon, not a sprint.

I love how Eugene Peterson rendered Matthew 7:24-27 in *The Message*:

> These words I speak to you are not incidental
> additions to your life, homeowner improvements
> to your standard of living. They are foundational
> words, words to build a life on. If you work these
> words into your life, you are like a smart carpenter

who built his house on solid rock. Rain poured
down, the river flooded, a tornado hit—but
nothing moved that house. It was fixed to the
rock.

But if you just use my words in Bible studies
and don't work them into your life, you are like a
stupid carpenter who built his house on the sandy
beach. When a storm rolled in and the waves came
up, it collapsed like a house of cards.

When we build our lives on the foundation of God's
love, nothing in life can destroy us. We're content in him,
no matter what comes. We won't rely on people or things for
our worth and identity. Building our lives on this foundation takes time. It takes investment. It takes digging deep
and rooting ourselves in his love. When we try to build our
relationships with God the quick and easy way, we lose out
on the strength and maturity that he longs to develop in us.
And without that strength and maturity, we're not going to
last when the waves come and the winds blow. Choosing to
be identified by God's love means choosing the only identity
in this world that will ever stand the test of time—the only
identity that will carry us through every circumstance.

Chapter 8

FUEL *for* *the* FIRE

For as long as I can remember, our entire Wilson clan has taken a trip to the High Sierras once a year for a family vacation. We get to forget about work, school, and the hustle and bustle of life and instead enjoy the artistry and wonder of God's creation, also known as the High Sierras and a place my family simply refers to as "Mammoth." This place is beautiful—lakes, rivers, streams, snowcapped mountains, and breathtaking views. Something about the outdoors ignites a sense of exploration and adventure. Many people say being outdoors brings them the closest to God's presence.

The outspoken abolitionist and poet Henry David Thoreau said it best:

> We need the tonic of wildness. . . . At the same time that we are earnest to explore and learn all things, we require that all things be mysterious and unexplorable, that land and sea be indefinitely wild, unsurveyed and unfathomed by us because unfathomable. We can never have enough of nature.[9]

Our trip to Mammoth took only about six hours via car ride, but when I was a young boy, it felt as though it was halfway around the world. Before leaving on this arduous adventure, I would make sure to pack all the essentials: snacks, Swiss Army pocketknife, original Game Boy, extra batteries, and more snacks. You know, the essentials. But no matter what I brought with me to help pass the time, I got bored about two hours into our adventure and constantly asked my father, "How much longer do you think until we get there?" Yeah, I was that kid. But I couldn't help myself. I was just excited to be on vacation with my family and to get out of school for a few weeks. I absolutely loved everything about spending time in Mammoth. It was the trip that my friends always asked me about when I came home, wanting to see all the pictures I had taken with my disposable camera. I still have a lot of those photos. I will cherish those memories forever.

Once at the campsites, which we had reserved almost a year out, chaos erupted as the different groups within our family began setting up tents, unloading RVs, and making the area feel like a piece of home. My grandfather usually fell asleep on a picnic table while the rest of us got to work. Not because he was lazy, but because hey, the guy deserved to rest. Technically none of us would be here without him. He was our tribe chief, and he'd been making the same trip every year for more than thirty years with his kids. He loved Mammoth: the place where everything in life was just perfect and the way it was meant to be. I still remember the year when he chased a bear out of our campsite in nothing but his underwear (I'll leave the details of that story to your imagination). My grandfather was the man. After he passed away, our family even mounted a small plaque on a tree at his favorite campsite. It's still there to this day.

Regardless of what everyone was doing upon arrival, we were all excited for the few weeks set aside to relax, refocus, and refuel as a family. These were the moments I'd remember for the rest of my life—moments that helped shape me into the man I am today. I dream of the day when my kids will be old enough for us to go to these mountains: to explore the wilderness, go fishing, and spend time in amazement and awe of God's creation and truly understand its totality.

One of my all-time favorite childhood activities in the mountains was starting the nightly campfire. It's no secret that all children are closet pyromaniacs. For some reason, kids and fire just go hand in hand. Fire is mesmerizing, to say the least, and it begs to be played with, poked at, and stared at until someone yells, "Stop playing with the fire! You're going to burn yourself, Jarrid!"

But I couldn't help it. It was fire, one of God's greatest creations (next to morning cartoons!). I was ten, and starting the family fire was a duty of honor. Getting to do so was almost a spiritual experience.

Lighting the fire was an art, and I loved every step of the process. I'd always start with some tiny wood shavings, stack a few logs on top of one another, and then add a small piece of paper to the bottom to finish it off. I'd imagine that my family was stranded in the middle of a desolate forest, cold and hungry, and for some reason I was the only one capable of igniting the flames that would bring us comfort. Not only was the fire going to bring our family warmth for the night, but it was also the way we would bring light to our campsite. And some nights, it's how we would even cook our food. It was a necessity.

In order to keep the fire roaring, I would find myself constantly adding more wood. Every twenty or thirty minutes, I'd add one log and then another and then another until we all decided it was time to head to bed. But even then, some nights we'd take turns adding logs overnight to keep the bears away. We were adding fuel to the fire in order to keep the fire alive.

Keep the Fire Burning

Just as we cannot rely on old logs to keep the fire burning, we also cannot rely on the faith of yesterday to keep our relationship with God flourishing today. And, as I heard an old preacher once say, we "can't ride the coattails of our father's faith." Keeping our passion alive for God is something that we have to choose to do each and every day. God's love is always available, but if we don't find ourselves constantly receiving that love and if we don't keep going back for more, our unique and beautiful relationship with God will diminish to embers, ceasing to produce anything of value. That's not a place any of us should want to be in, especially as people commissioned with the incredible task of sharing the gospel with all nations and all people. God has provided us with everything we need to keep our faith in him active and vibrant, but we have to make the decision to receive it and apply it. I think we'd all be surprised to know how many people are handed God's wisdom and guidance but don't utilize it.

We must always be on the lookout to add more nourishment to the fire pits that are our spiritual lives. God's love fuels not only our own spiritual lives but also everything we do to love others and make a difference in the world for Jesus' sake. It's like the great John Wesley once said: "Get on fire for God and men will come and see you burn." And that's exactly what we're called to do. Without our hearts ablaze in faith, we're no good to the cause of Christ. Without our souls on fire with love, we're nothing more than darkness. And that's exactly where Satan wants us to be. We cannot do anything in our own love, because our own love isn't really love at all. Only through the power and fuel of God's love can we make a difference in this world.

But what does adding fuel to the fire of your faith really look like? Well, the best way I can think of putting it is that the relationship you have with God should be like a flourishing and vibrant marriage. Your relationship with God is single-handedly the most important relationship you will ever find yourself in. You should take it very seriously, and you can't afford to drift away. You must do everything you can to make sure your relationship with God stays healthy, fiery, and passionate. Because if not, your relationship with God will just become a statistic—you'll just be another Christian going through life with no real purpose or meaning. But keeping the fire going is easier than you may think.

In January of 2014, I wrote a blog post titled "I'm Dating Someone Even Though I'm Married."[10] Yes, the title may have seemed a bit crazy. But it was the best way I could think of to stress the conviction I felt to pursue my wife as I did when we were dating. I wanted to regain and deepen that spark, passion, and desire. I wanted to go back to that feeling of butterflies in my stomach, the nervousness that made my palms sweat. I had unintentionally lost it. The reason for writing the post was hard for me to admit, but it was something I needed to say—and something that a lot of couples needed to hear.

My wife and I realized that the daily routine of marriage can set in pretty quickly, and if you're not careful, that exciting and new relationship can accidentally get put on the back burner, while work and other things are made more of a priority. That's where I was. And it wasn't at all on purpose. Nobody sets out to do this when he or she gets married. My way of showing my wife I loved her had become working hard and providing for her financially. Those are both really good things. But I'd become so focused on them that I'd stopped pursuing her heart in the ways she desired. I stopped doing all the awesome things I once did when we were dating and engaged. The things that showed her I was willing to go out of my way to express my love for her. She yearned for me to pursue her, because it showed her that I was still interested in who she was, even though we were already married. That I was choosing her over and over again despite the fact that we already had rings on our fingers. I quickly realized how important it is to constantly invest in my relationship with my wife, regardless of how long we've been together. That I can't just rely on the actions and words and intimacy of yesterday to fulfill what needs to be done today. The pursuit should never end.

That seems like a pretty obvious statement, but you'd be surprised how many couples needed to confront this truth head-on as much as I did.

What I said struck a chord. Millions of people read the post and really resonated with the idea of relentlessly pursuing their spouse. In fact, the post gained so much exposure that it was featured on numerous news stations and media outlets, and Juli and I were even flown in as guests for Steve Harvey's daytime TV show. It was a pretty surreal experience. I think the words resonated with so many because deep down we all want to be loved and pursued.

The idea of pursuing your spouse should be in the forefront of your mind. Why? Because you'll never learn enough about the person you are with. There is always more to learn, more to experience, and more to adventure with each other.

And the same is true for a relationship with God. See where I'm going with this? The similarities are quite extraordinary. We must live in constant pursuit of our God, constantly longing to know and love him more, so that we may then fuel our own lives with his love, truly loving him and loving others. It comes full circle.

God relentlessly pursues you every day, and he deserves the same in return. Pursuing God's love isn't a "have to"; it's a "get to." It's an undeserved blessing. Discovering the wonder of God's love isn't a onetime affair but instead a daily process. And the daily pursuit of God can come in many shapes and forms. Prayer, worship, servanthood, and studying God's Word are all ways to pursue God's heart and find rest in his love. Doing these things in selflessness and humility is the key to engaging in a fruitful relationship with Christ. All of God's most influential and righteous followers were those who relentlessly pursued him. Yes, they may have all had some hiccups along the way, but the pursuit nonetheless defined their lives. Only the man or woman who chases after God will come to actually know him and dwell with him and not just be a spectator.

God deserves our relentless pursuit: a pursuit that jumps hurdles and goes above and beyond. We must live in a posture of yearning for the love and righteousness of God as if it were the first time we'd ever taken notice of it. The fire that is our relationship with God must be fueled daily and kept roaring so that no matter what obstacles we face in life, God's love will propel us forward.

A strong relationship, no matter who it's with, cannot exist without quality time, communication, humility, honesty, and transparency. My relationship with my wife won't last unless she and I continue to pursue each other. Just look at how many marriages in today's world end up in divorce, all because individuals claim that their relationship just fizzled out. Or that the spark just isn't there anymore. Or that they love each other but just aren't "in love" with each other anymore. This happens because the husband and wife stop pursuing each other, stop putting the other person first, and stop living a life dedicated to knowing the other person more than the day before. Your relationships give what you put into them. And our relationship with God is really no different. Every day we must allow room for God's will to take center stage and our selfish desires to take a back seat. That's the only way it will work.

Clinging to Jesus fuels the Christian life. It keeps the fire burning. There is no substitute. No replacement. No generic alternative. We aren't destined to make a life for ourselves through ourselves, but instead through the love of Jesus. Jesus alone is the reason we live and breathe. He alone is the reason we are allowed to experience all the vast wonders this world has to offer. Everything we do in life is derived from the power and majesty of his love.

Everything we do should be to glorify God, to be awakened and fully alive through Jesus Christ: "When you were dead in your sins and in the uncircumcision of your flesh,

God made you alive with Christ. He forgave us all our sins" (Colossians 2:13, NIV).

In his letter to the Colossians, Paul didn't just say that we were "empty" or living meaningless lives. If only that were the case. What he actually said is that we were dead, that we don't have anything figured out or put together. Now for the good news: God made us "alive with Christ." He took something totally lifeless—me, you—and made it alive. I don't know about you, but that makes me excited! That's the kind of truth that can change lives—change entire cultures. At the heart of this fire: Jesus. The *love* you receive from God isn't dependent on how good of a person you are. Prayer, worship, and obtaining knowledge don't earn us the love of God—these things put us in the posture to receive the love he so desperately wants to give us. He craves opportunities to bless us. You're *already* loved beyond measure. Accept it, embrace it, and let it fuel your life to the fullest extent. You will never regret doing so.

I remember being confused the first time I heard this. Mostly because I was perplexed that God didn't want anything from me before I could obtain his love for me. It was already there, and that blew me away. To think that the creator of the universe already loves us despite what we do or don't do, say or don't say, pray or don't pray. That truth showed me how gracious and compassionate he really is. It's a love that has no bounds.

One of the first books I ever read as a believer was *The Pursuit of God* by A. W. Tozer. Something he said still shakes my soul today: "To have found God and still to pursue Him is a paradox of love."[11] The idea of finding God and choosing to pursue him may sound silly or like a waste of time, but it's actually the truest example of showing your love for God. It's like the world's greatest game of hide-and-seek. We should continue to chase him as if we've never found him.

For much of my past, I did the opposite of this. I constantly found myself trying to do things in my own strength, pursuing myself and my desires instead of pursuing God. And I was so lonely. The act of pursuing God is the act of pursuing love itself. And an active relationship with God is the only remedy for your soul's longing for connection and purpose. Trust me when I say that it's the only thing that can truly bring you fulfillment in life. The world around you will constantly try to trick you into believing that other things out there can fuel your soul and give you the life you truly desire. But nothing else can. Nothing else will ever be able to. Only in chasing after the things of God can you discover your true self. The pursuit will refine you, mold you, and help shape you into the person God has called you to be. Like a rock that falls into a creek bed, you will eventually find your jagged edges made smooth.

Now, maybe for you, the thought of reading a Bible or even praying makes you cringe. Or maybe you've believed in God for as long as you can remember, but the wondrous life of a Christ follower is still not what it's cracked up to be. Jesus, Christianity, and the Bible are nothing more than a part of your daily routine, one that doesn't fuel the way you live or the person you are becoming. I get it. I used to be that person. I used to think Christianity was boring, a hands-down waste of time. When I was younger, I was never a fan of going to church or getting dropped off at yet another youth-group event. It all seemed to be pointless and irrelevant. But then I actually experienced Jesus for who he really is and not who I assumed him to be. I dropped my pride and finally let God in. This didn't happen overnight, but with persistence and humility my relationship with God truly started to grow and my edges began to smooth out. My eyes have finally been opened to the presence of God, and my life is now fueled by his glorious love.

If you think Christianity is boring, then you haven't met Jesus. When you truly encounter the consuming love of Jesus, your life is anything but mundane and stale. The love and power of Jesus are too marvelous to walk away from once you taste them. Worship is exhilarating, reading the Bible is fascinating, and prayer is a conversation with God that you can't seem to stay away from. The Bible says that we are sanctified (set apart) by the blood of Christ, and we must realize that we cannot truly digest this truth and not find the eternal joy that comes along with it.

The Bible paints a very clear picture of what happens when someone belongs to Christ and has discovered the wonder of God's love. The old fades away and a new life begins. Only through Jesus can we truly come alive in the life and the community we were created for. Life in Christ encompasses the totality of Christ himself, which characteristically is anything but monotonous and mind-numbing.

> Because of his great love for us, God, who is rich in mercy, made us alive with Christ even when we were dead in transgressions—it is by grace you have been saved. And God raised us up with Christ and seated us with him in the heavenly realms in Christ Jesus, in order that in the coming ages he might show the incomparable riches of his grace, expressed in his kindness to us in Christ Jesus. For it is by grace you have been saved, through faith—and this is not from yourselves, it is the gift of God—not by works, so that no one can boast. For we are God's handiwork, created in Christ Jesus to do good works, which God prepared in advance for us to do.
>
> EPHESIANS 2:4-10, NIV

A life in Christ brings purpose, restoration, grace, and eternal identity. It fuels us beyond imagination. The adventure that awaits a follower of Jesus is one this world simply cannot come close to matching. Every day is a new experience, a new facet of God's glory, and another opportunity to deepen your personal relationship with the Creator. There's always room for growth, which means there's always room for adventure. And the adventure of living in God's love means taking the fire we've been given and setting it free.

Pass the Torch

You might be wondering, *Okay, so how do I love God? What does that even mean? Do I sit around thinking good, "loving" thoughts about him? Or do I love him through actions? How does it work?* Jesus gives us a very clear answer. In Matthew 25, he tells the people gathered around him that one day he will come back and say to those who fed the hungry, showed hospitality to the stranger, clothed the naked, cared for the sick, and visited the imprisoned: "Truly I tell you, whatever you did for one of the least of these brothers and sisters of mine, you did for me" (verse 40, NIV). The gospel of Jesus is complex and full of layers, but the application we are to follow is nothing more than basic direction: Love God, love people. Or as Dwight L. Moody framed it,

> If we have got the true love of God shed abroad in our hearts we will show it in our lives. We will not have to go up and down the earth proclaiming it. We will show it in everything we say or do.[12]

By loving others in the most simple and hands-on ways, we also love God. We are bringing glory to his name, glory to the Cross, and glory to his Son, Jesus. We fuel the fire even more. Loving him isn't an abstract exercise of the mind. It's an action that takes place through our relationships and interactions with other people—it's taking the fire to others.

I think of it a little bit like a wildfire. It's not a perfect analogy—wildfires, after all, can be scary and destructive—but wildfires can also have an incredible purpose: They burn up what's dead in a forest and make way for new life that wouldn't yet be able to flourish. My uncle is a firefighter who spent most of his early career working with a team that fights California forest fires. He'd be the first to tell you that wildfires, especially ones with the wind to their backs, are unrelenting. They have the power to climb hills and jump across interstates. And the more fuel a fire has, the wilder it gets, the faster it moves, and the larger of an area it will affect and consume. The same is true about our relationships with God and our effectiveness as Christians.

Loving others by extending the love of God through our actions, words, and everyday lives is not only contagious but also brings life to those giving and those on the receiving end. It lifts them up to new heights. God's love is like a wildfire—expansive, consuming, and reckless. And with the Holy Spirit to our backs, unstoppable. God created his people in his image so that they could love, help those in need, and expand the great commission to all nations, as we see in the New Testament. Our calling as Christians is to love those we come into contact with, share the message of Jesus, and worship with all that we are, no matter the circumstance.

It's not always easy, but remember this: We were created to love. It's our purpose in life. To love others, making much of Jesus' name. And with Jesus, it's possible. As minister Samuel Chadwick said,

> Spirit-filled souls are ablaze for God. They love with a love that glows. They believe with a faith that kindles. They serve with a devotion that consumes. They hate sin with a fierceness that burns. They rejoice with a joy that radiates. Love is perfected in the Fire of God.[13]

This fire is all-consuming—everything near it gets drawn in. When we're close to this fire—when we open ourselves up to learning about Jesus—we can't help but be pulled into it and want others to feel its warm embrace. We love because he loved us first. We forgive because he forgave us first. We serve others because Jesus served us first. Our love is because of God. Our servanthood is because of God. Our being is because of God. When we model ourselves after this truth, we allow God's love to spark the power into our lives that keeps us moving forward. Jesus, and only Jesus, can provide us with the fuel we need to love others well. When we truly encounter Jesus, we will never be without that fuel.

Chapter 9

The GREATEST
of THESE

The reality of God's love for you may be something you've heard countless times. But don't miss this: Reflecting on his love and what it's done for us is such an important foundation for our spiritual lives. As we learn to truly breathe in God's love, we are equipped and motivated to show that love to others. Because what good is acquiring this love for ourselves if we're not going to share it? God's love isn't selfish; it begs to be breathed out to others.

We all need to wrestle with what we should do with this immense love we've been given. It may look different for you than for me, but our call to breathe out remains the same. If we're supposed to be following Jesus and living like him, and Jesus showed radical love to everyone he came across no matter what, then what would it look like for us to love like Jesus? His love goes out of its way to be shown, known, and given.

God's Word talks a lot about love, but there's one passage that paints the most vivid picture of what God's love looks like in our lives and what it should look like as we take it to others: 1 Corinthians 13. And this passage starts out with a pretty strong statement about the importance of a life defined by love: "If I could speak all the languages of earth and of angels, but didn't love others, I would only be a noisy gong or a clanging cymbal" (verse 1).

I'm no stranger to 1 Corinthians 13, but one time when I read it, the word *cymbal* stood out to me in a way it never had before. Dwelling on this word gave me insight into how life looks when we don't equip our words and actions with love.

A short time later, I found myself delivering a message on this passage. It was during an election season, a time when malicious attacks and finger-pointing seemed to run rampant not only among the candidates but also among everyday people. The timing, I thought, was no coincidence. The middle of strife is the best time to talk about love.

I started my message by explaining the reality of God's love for our lives—how God himself is love and how our duty as Christians is to show love to the world. At this point, everybody was still nodding in agreement. But the moment I started asking people to evaluate their lives to see if they were following through by truly loving those around them, everyone's demeanor began to change. I was the first to admit that I don't always reflect God's love. I didn't want anyone to think I had it all together. Because I didn't. And I don't.

I then began to unpack the way we should be treating one another, not only in person but online—through comments, posts, tweets, and replies. It's easy to stay civil when we're face-to-face with someone, but our behavior often changes behind the safety of an online profile and screen. We live in a world full of clashing opinions and beliefs, and I often wonder if we fall short in living out love to those we disagree with.

I took a step back on the stage, grabbed a drumstick, and then pulled up a cymbal and stand to the left of my table. I paused for a moment. Then, still teaching my message on love, I abruptly changed my words into rude and cruel remarks, crashing the drumstick onto the cymbal while continuing as if nothing were happening.

"My opinion on immigration is . . ." *crashing cymbals*

"My opinion on politics is . . ." *crashing cymbals*

"My opinion on marriage is . . ." *crashing cymbals*

"My opinion on abortion is . . ." *crashing cymbals*

When I stepped out from behind the cymbal stand, I asked if everyone had heard everything I had said in the last few minutes. Some of them laughed. Some of them said, "Amen." Some of them still had their hands over their ears in case I smacked the cymbal again. They'd gotten the point.

If we aren't speaking in love, nobody is going to hear what we are saying, no matter how truthful or important it might be. They're not going to listen to us or respect us. And yes, our world is certainly full of crashing cymbals, many of whom don't know God's love, so the urge to act this way makes sense. But many of us who call ourselves Christians fall into the trap of sharing our opinions in a way that is unloving.

We can't love others without the love of God. The love of God is kind and compassionate. No matter how deep or truthful we may think our words are, if we're speaking and acting without love, no one can hear us. Anything said without love isn't worth saying at all. Anything done without love isn't worth doing at all. And you can imagine what it must feel like for those being criticized by people who think they are doing so in "love," when really it's just out of a misplaced sense of pride or superiority or judgment. Those being criticized hear nothing but the crashing of cymbals. But the moment love enters the picture, the clanging stops. Our voices become clear. Our words become valuable again.

Paul continued:

> If I had the gift of prophecy, and if I understood all
> of God's secret plans and possessed all knowledge,
> and if I had such faith that I could move mountains,
> but didn't love others, I would be nothing. If I gave
> everything I have to the poor and even sacrificed
> my body, I could boast about it; but if I didn't love
> others, I would have gained nothing.
>
> 1 CORINTHIANS 13:2-3

Without love, nothing matters—not speaking in tongues or having the gift of prophecy or possessing all knowledge or even having faith that could move mountains. We could know all sorts of things about God, listen to all the sermons we can get our hands on, write books, be the best worship leader or teacher or preacher—but if we do any of those things without love, nothing matters. It's all a waste of time.

It's possible to act spiritually and say you follow God but be nothing more than a fake, a Pharisee, a love-heretic. God sees people doing it daily.

Without love, we can't fulfill God's calling for our lives. Without love, we can't engage in the relationship that God yearns for. And without love, we can't truly reflect God's image at all. Try to think of a single person who is doing incredible things for the Kingdom of God without the love of God. That person doesn't exist. Life without the love of God will let you down and lead you in the wrong direction. We were meant for a life empowered by love, in which God's love affects every little thing we do.

Paul continued his love chorus, showing us exactly what this kind of love is supposed to look like—and what it doesn't look like.

> Love is patient and kind. Love is not jealous or boastful or proud or rude. It does not demand its own way. It is not irritable, and it keeps no record of being wronged. It does not rejoice about injustice but rejoices whenever the truth wins out. Love never gives up, never loses faith, is always hopeful, and endures through every circumstance.
>
> Prophecy and speaking in unknown languages and special knowledge will become useless. But love will last forever! Now our knowledge is partial and incomplete, and even the gift of prophecy

reveals only part of the whole picture! But when
the time of perfection comes, these partial things
will become useless.

When I was a child, I spoke and thought
and reasoned as a child. But when I grew up,
I put away childish things. Now we see things
imperfectly, like puzzling reflections in a mirror,
but then we will see everything with perfect clarity.
All that I know now is partial and incomplete, but
then I will know everything completely, just as
God now knows me completely.

1 CORINTHIANS 13:4-12

Love is patience and kindness—no jealousy or boasting
or rudeness or selfishness. Anything that keeps a record of
wrongs or rejoices at injustice is not love. Love is said to
endure every circumstance that life throws its way. If we
plan on living a life of love, this is how we're supposed
to live.

I've always wondered about that last part of this group of
verses. The spot where Paul said, "Three things will last forever—faith, hope, and love—and the greatest of these is love"
(verse 13). What does it mean that love is greater than faith
or hope? Consider this: Love encapsulates faith and hope.
Faith and hope make up the DNA of love.

"The greatest of these is love" because the greatest of these
is God—and God is love. God is the essence of love itself.

Without God—without love—we don't have faith or hope. And because of God—because of our faith and hope—love should be the mission of our lives. Love is a weapon against the darkness and sorrow of the world. Love should be the anthem of our souls.

Love One Another

If love is the heartbeat of God, encapsulating everything about our faith and hope, then it shouldn't be a surprise that the idea of offering that love to everyone we come across permeates Scripture. In fact, the word *love* can be found hundreds of times in the Bible. In the New Living Translation, it appears 759 times. That's impressive. And let's not forget the command to love our enemies that many find hard to swallow:

> Love your enemies, do good to them, and lend to them without expecting to get anything back. Then your reward will be great, and you will be children of the Most High, because he is kind to the ungrateful and wicked.
> LUKE 6:35, NIV

None of us really wants to love our enemies. If someone has hurt us, the last thing we want to do is to do good to that person. But that's what God calls us to. And that's what a woman named Mary Johnson did in the face of profound horror: the murder of her only child.[14]

At first, Mary hated the young man who murdered her son. Several years into his prison sentence, Mary decided to visit him. She soon saw that the boy she had met so many years ago was no longer that animal she once called him. So what did she do? She forgave him. "Unforgiveness is like cancer. It will eat you from the inside out," she said in an interview with CBS.[15]

She could have stayed bitter, withdrawn, and angry. She could have held on to her hatred for her son's killer, and frankly, nobody would have judged her for it. But she didn't.

She continued to visit with the young man until he was released from prison seventeen years after being convicted, and then took him under her wing, becoming someone he called his second mom.

Love conquered the hate she had in her heart for her son's killer. And this is what it means to love your enemy. Not just the people who annoy us, not just the people we don't feel like loving—but the people who have affected our lives in painful and destructive ways. I know Satan hates hearing stories like Mary's. Because once again, love won. And Mary's story has encouraged others to show love and forgiveness toward their loved ones' killers. Love is contagious. And it has the power to overcome so much darkness.

Our job as followers of Jesus is to reflect an image of

love to everyone around us—the same love that Jesus showed on a splintered plank of wood known as the cross. Without love we are meaningless. Without love we are without Jesus. Without love, the gospel isn't truly the gospel at all. Jesus himself is the image we must seek to reflect, and our mission is to love because he first loved us.

We may not have to live out the extreme kind of love Jesus talked about in Luke 6, but we are called to love in every situation we face, no matter how easy or how hard. And every day we are given opportunities to show love. It doesn't take much effort at all. Just think about how many people you see throughout your day—while getting coffee, filling up your gas tank, getting lunch, going to the bank, running errands. We encounter literally thousands of people whom we have the opportunity to love. And love is more about availability and less about skill or qualification. If you make yourself fully available to be used by God, you'll constantly find yourself in the midst of opportunities to show his love.

I can't begin to tell you how many people my wife and I eventually find ourselves calling friends simply because we said hi, held a door open for them at a restaurant, or offered encouragement in the midst of their bad day. Little acts of love make a big difference, but you'll never know until you extend it. God's love brings together people who would otherwise never spend time with one another. We need to seize every opportunity we can to reflect an image of love and kindness throughout our day and let God take care of the rest. We're just the messengers. God is the orchestrator.

As Christians, we must learn to exude the image of God's love through every facet of our lives. There's no such thing as a private relationship with God. Personal, yes. Private, no. The biblical text is clear that our lives should be public, daily shows of God's many beautiful characteristics. We're not called to be flashy, but we are called to be proud of who we represent and call Lord.

> You are the light of the world—like a city on a hilltop that cannot be hidden. No one lights a lamp and then puts it under a basket. Instead, a lamp is placed on a stand, where it gives light to everyone in the house. In the same way, let your good deeds shine out for all to see, so that everyone will praise your heavenly Father.
>
> MATTHEW 5:14-16

Just as we wouldn't light a lamp and then cover it—diluting its sole purpose—as Christians, we aren't supposed to keep the hope of Jesus hidden from the public eye. Not showing the love of Jesus to others would completely hamper us from fulfilling the great commission: to "make disciples of all the nations, baptizing them in the name of the Father and the Son and the Holy Spirit" (Matthew 28:19).

It just doesn't make any sense to stay quiet in a world that parades darkness and deceit. Our faith was made to be public and outspoken. To be shared. To be discussed with those we come across. We are called to be shining examples of Christ in all that we do, no matter what we do, no matter where we are, no matter who we come into contact with.

Now, I understand strategic evangelism in countries where Christianity is illegal, but we, as Americans, really have no excuse to be silent. I'm not saying you need to be on the street corner with a banner that says I Love Jesus!, but I am saying you should have no issue letting people know who you've given your life to. We're called to live unashamed to the fullest extent.

> I am not ashamed of this Good News about Christ.
> It is the power of God at work, saving everyone who
> believes—the Jew first and also the Gentile.
> ROMANS 1:16

When our lives get caught up in the beauty of the gospel, we realize our existence is no longer about us. Our vocation as Christ followers is to share the alluring and jaw-dropping beauty of the gospel.

Chapter 10

PREPAID LOVE

If we dwell in this incredible love of God and believe what he's told us through his Word, we shouldn't want to or be able to contain it. God's love should overflow. It should be so in and through us that it can't help but spill out onto the people around us. And love—true, actual, without-strings-attached love—can change lives. You never know what a single act of kindness could do for someone. You never know what one action of love could actually mean for someone going through a tough time.

I guess I never really understood that until I met Tom.

It was a hot and muggy summer day in Southern California. I was visiting the mall for some reason I can't remember—probably to get a new pair of shoes or meet up with some friends. As I headed back toward my car, I saw something leaning against a tree to my right—a person trying to find relief in the shade. He was an older gentleman, holding a small sign that read Anything Helps! Normally I would have handed him a five-dollar bill and continued on my merry way, but God had other plans.

The man sat there in the blazing sun, wearing tattered

clothes, shoes that looked almost worn through, and a back-pack that seemed too small to really be useful. His eyes were somber, his skin looked like leather, and he seemed fragile. It was easy to see that he was homeless and in need of some help. I suspected that he hadn't had a warm meal in a long time.

I had probably been to that mall a thousand times, and while I had seen many others looking for a small handout, I didn't recognize this man. As I continued toward my car, I tried to justify ignoring him. It's not that I didn't care about him or his needs; I just told myself that I was too busy to stop and that I'd make sure to pray for him later. It's such a silly and immature response, especially for someone who calls himself a follower of Jesus.

We all do this, don't we? We yearn for God to use us, but then we justify why we can't engage in the opportunities he sends our way because they're not quite convenient. When life is relatively easy and comfortable, as it is for so many of us who are Christians in America, we tend to lean more on our comforts than on the love of God. We want Jesus but on our time. We want to be used but only in ways we feel comfortable with. We want to change the world but need to take care of our own needs first. However, living out of love pushes us out of our comfort zone. Suddenly, we start seeing people as God sees them—and we can't just pass by. But while I tried to get to my car without addressing the man leaning against the tree, something powerful impressed on my heart and redirected my steps toward him.

"Hey there!" I smiled and extended my hand. The man looked at me with a little confusion and said, "Hello there, sir." He seemed to struggle to stretch his hand to me, and I noticed how mangled and malformed his hands looked. He later told me it was because of a combination of war injuries and progressive muscular dystrophy. I asked him for his name and how his day was. I figured that talking to him was good enough for today's mission—when I was done, I could be on my way back home and feel good about what I'd done. But God told me I wasn't going to get off that easy. My heart needed to change perspective.

"My name is Tom," the man said. "It's short for Thomas."

"Hey, my first name is Thomas too!" I told him. "But I go by my middle name, Jarrid. It's part of a family tradition." We both felt a small connection in sharing a first name, and I could see that something as simple as that created a bit of trust between us.

Tom was almost eighty years old and had been homeless for the last twenty of those years. He lost his job shortly after returning home from the war. Years later his wife died of cancer, and they had no children he could rely on for help. He was alone, and his only option was to live on the streets. It broke me to hear this.

"I've lived this way for a long time, but I'm getting too old to do this now," Tom said. He explained that he received a small check in the mail each month for his time serving in the military during the Vietnam War but that it wasn't enough for him to rent even the worst of apartments in Southern California. He couldn't move to a different state because of his health and age. "I'm kind of stuck," he said, his eyes half-closed.

I asked him what I could do to help. "New clothes? Some money? A place to sleep for the night?"

Thomas said, "You know what? Because of my health, I could really use one of those cheap prepaid phones for emergencies. Nothing fancy. Other than that, I really am okay until I find a place cheap enough to rent."

"Perfect! I can do that," I said. And I made my way back into the mall, where I purchased a ten-dollar prepaid phone, activated it, and then got him some new socks, a few shirts, and some other necessities I thought he could use. After I had made my way back to the big tree he was lying under, he looked at me with a big smile and said, "What on earth did you get?"

I put my number in the phone, handed it to him, and then explained the other things I had got him. I asked if there was anything else I could do or somewhere I could take him. I offered to let him shower at my small apartment. He insisted he had everything he needed and that his little makeshift tent underneath the freeway was perfectly fine for the time being. He had friends there, and they took care of one another. Before we said our good-byes, I prayed over him and told him to call me if he ever needed anything. I promised him I would help in any way I could, and after hugging it out, we said our good-byes and went our separate ways.

A month later, I found myself once again at the mall. I had been there a few times since running into Tom, but he was nowhere to be found. As I walked up to the front doors, I passed the tree where Tom had found comfort in the shade, and I decided I'd take a moment to relax and sit there myself. I prayed for him and his health and asked God if he could give me some way to make sure he was all right. *Maybe he's found an apartment*, I thought hopefully. Then, worriedly, *Maybe he got hurt.* I had texted and called him a few times after we had initially met, but he never answered. I assumed he was all right and he would know to call me if anything drastic happened.

I got up and started to make my way toward the mall when suddenly I saw a scrawny, gray-haired man approaching. It was Tom. He was wearing the hat and one of the shirts I had given him. "Tom!" I called across the parking lot. He didn't recognize me until I was about ten feet away.

"Hey, you! I was wondering when I'd run into you again," he said. I explained that I was wondering the same thing and asked how he was doing.

He shook his head. "You'll never guess what happened," he told me. "The night you got me that cell phone and clothes, I had a heart attack underneath the bridge. None of my friends were back yet, and I didn't know what to do. Then I remembered you had got me that phone, and I dialed 911."

I literally had no words. *You have got to be kidding me*, I thought.

"I told the operator where I was, and they picked me up within a few minutes. I was in the hospital for more than a week. I almost died that night, Jarrid. That phone saved my life. You saved my life, and I have no idea how to repay you."

"Repay me?" I said. "I'm just glad you're all right, man! This is a total God thing. Don't thank me. Thank him."

"I know." He laughed. "I just want to thank you for noticing me. You could have ignored me that day, but you didn't."

Tom then told me he'd gotten into a program in Orange County that helped homeless veterans find affordable housing. Because of his age and health condition, he had been placed in a home within a matter of days.

My connection with Tom is one of those experiences that will stay with me for the rest of my life. Why? Because it showed me, so vividly, how a single act of living out God's love—something as simple as noticing someone, stopping, and giving them a ten-dollar prepaid phone—can be the difference between life and death. Every act of love has a drastic impact on the world around us. And every act of love is an act against death.

By following God and loving the people around us, we're offering them life-giving oxygen: the chance to see and know God's love for themselves and those around them.

You never know what people are going through, how broken they are, or how in need of a simple "hello" they may be. Love doesn't have to be extravagant. It just has to be love. Remember, when the love of God fills our lives, it should overflow. Every ounce of who we are should yearn to help and love those around us.

When we learn to put aside our own selfish agendas and comforts and instead embrace God's agenda of love, the world will become a better place, one filled with compassion and understanding. I'm reminded of a quote by Francis Chan: "I believe He wants us to love others so much that we go to extremes to help them."[16]

We all need to ask ourselves some questions: What are we doing to show the world a tangible and active example of God's love? Has the love of God so filled our lives that we can't help but show it to others? Are we taking advantage of the opportunities God has put before us to love our neighbors, or are we ignoring people in need because of selfishness and our desire for comfort? These are tough questions. But living out love should define our lives when we grasp God's love for us. Love should change the way we interact with the people around us. It should change everything about us.

I don't share about Tom to try to convince you that I'm some sort of incredible person who has got this love thing figured out. But I wanted to show you that when we elevate God's yearning to love on a pedestal higher than ourselves, incredibly beautiful things can happen.

I'm struck by a beautiful underlying meaning in Tom's prepaid phone that served as lifeline: Jesus' death on the cross paid and prepaid for any debts we owe. His death and resurrection are our lifelines. Jesus went to the cross knowing we don't deserve that kind of forgiveness, but love meant that he did it anyway. And because of this, we are to be the same kind of love to others. No matter where you are or what it may look like, just love. Take time to pause and extend a hand to people who may need it. Leave money in the mailbox of that person who can't make his or her rent. Pay for the lunch of the family in line behind you. Fix the flat tire for the person on the side of the road. Buy a cheap little phone for someone who needs a lifeline. Do it all with love. You never know what something as simple as a conversation or a prepaid cell phone can do for someone's life. Opportunities are every-where. Grab hold of them.

Chapter 11

WHAT LOVE
looks LIKE

When Jesus began his ministry here on earth, he didn't take the route you might expect. He didn't take advantage of his power as the almighty Alpha and Omega. He had nothing but the clothes on his back and words of anthemic proportion, and he did what everyone was least expecting from the Messiah. He didn't try to rub shoulders with powerful influencers or rich politicians to gain popularity and status. He didn't set out to build his Kingdom from the top down or go out of his way to try to sell the fact that he was the Son of God. He didn't brag about who he was, try to trick individuals into joining him, or use Jedi mind control to gain a following. His approach was gutsy and raw and grassroots. He started from the bottom. Jesus went to "the least of these" (Matthew 25:40)—the people who were the absolute last on anybody's list of Most Influential People.

Take his followers, for example: the twelve disciples. These guys weren't philanthropists, social influencers, or scholars; they were blue-collar boys, fishermen and tradesmen. It's not that the disciples weren't smart; they just didn't have the societal ranking that people would expect. And

Jesus didn't stop there. He chose to do life with the hurting and brokenhearted, the oddballs, the black sheep, and the misfits—people who continually needed his attention, help, encouragement, and forgiveness. Prostitutes, drunks, swindlers, thieves, adulterers, tax collectors—these are just a few of society's castoffs whom Jesus truly and deeply and wholeheartedly loved.

God's Son came to spend time and die for sinners, the messed up, and those who are sick. How incredibly humbling and beautiful. The perfect Savior wanted to spend time with imperfect people, and he did this knowing he'd be there to witness firsthand their struggles and misfortunes. But he loved them—despite the hardships, despite the messiness.

Love may be like oxygen, but that doesn't mean the air around us is always clean and abundant. It doesn't mean that love is always going to be easy. If you've ever climbed a mountain or stood at high elevation, then you know that gasping feeling—that raspy, winded, stretching-your-lungs-out feeling of trying to get in a good breath. It hurts. It's not the kind of oxygen we wish we had. It's not the easy kind of breath we need. But without those much-needed breaths, no matter how hard they are, our lungs would deflate and our hearts would cease. Don't believe me? Try to hold your breath for ten minutes and see what happens. (I'm just kidding. Don't do that.)

That's how it is with love. It's not always going to be simple to love others. It's not always going to be convenient or without hardship and deprivation. But it's still how we breathe. It's still the very thing that keeps us alive in the spirit of God. Because when we breathe out love to others for the sake of glorifying God, we in turn breathe in the love that God has for us.

We've been assigned the arduous and humbling task of showing love to all people, and this includes those we consider our worst enemies, those who live differently, those whom we don't believe deserve love, those whom we think are too far gone. Murderers, rapists, thieves, cheats, liars, and even terrorists are just a few of the people we are called to show love and grace to. Why? Because these people are no better or worse than you and me. That may be a hard pill to swallow, but it's just the truth. We're supposed to show love to everyone, no matter who they are or what they've done—because Jesus died for all of us. This may sound extreme, but it's just love.

I firmly believe you can radically love people without approving or affirming their decisions, no matter how radical those decisions may be. That kind of love takes time. It's not something we can practice today and skip out on tomorrow. When we agree to get our elbows dirty with Jesus' brand of love, we agree to play the long game, even on the days we don't feel like it. And if we want guidance on how we should treat people who are different from us, Jesus is the perfect example:

- He loved people who were different from him.
- He ate with people who were different from him.

- He served people who were different from him.
- He befriended people who were different from him.

That's just who Jesus is. So many times I find myself reading the Bible and noticing Jesus do things that seem so simple in nature but actually have such a huge impact. Over and over again, Jesus used himself as an example of what to say, how to say it, when to say it, and whom to say it to. He does this for a reason. And it's because he wants us to be like him. He wants us to follow his lead by doing what he did and saying what he said. People aren't always going to understand our reflection of Jesus. The Bible tells us not even the Pharisees understood why he was doing what he was doing half the time. Jesus' way of living and loving was so foreign to them that they couldn't think of any other way to respond than "That's wrong." But it wasn't. Nothing he did was ever wrong. But he did spend a lot of quality time with people who were doing the wrong things, and that's what I believe led the Pharisees and religious rulers to be so confused. He was spending time with people who were doing bad things.

But that's the thing . . . if you call yourself a Christian, then you're called to be like Jesus. And you don't have to agree with someone's lifestyle in order to spend time together, love that person, or show you care. You don't have to have the same beliefs to have dinner together. You can befriend people who are different from you without being a complete and insensitive jerk. And this can lead you to some radical things.

My wife and I actually decided together that it would be best if I stepped down from a job in order to follow Jesus this way. We dropped everything without a backup plan because we felt the organization wasn't loving a group of people the way Jesus calls us to love, regardless of our beliefs on the topic. Of course, we sought the wise counsel of close friends, pastors, and mentors to make sure we were hearing God correctly. And all of them unanimously told me with complete confidence, "You can't be there. That's not who you are. It's time to part ways." It was heartbreaking, but my wife and I knew, without hesitation, that it was time for me to leave because we'd rather step out in faith and have no clue where God might have us next than be part of withholding love and grace from people. A paycheck and health insurance should not come before relationships and following God, especially when core convictions are involved. Living out the love of Jesus means following him wherever he calls us, no matter how hard it might be. And trust me, it was hard and confusing and a little discouraging in the beginning. But even a month after we had stepped down, God had already begun showing us how right the decision really was. The reality is, sometimes God needs you to move in order for the fullness of his blessing to come upon your life. And that's exactly what happened with us.

Life is too short to live without love and compassion. Jesus didn't carry around a list of everyone's faults and failures. He didn't stand on the street corner and yell at people who were different from him or didn't quite understand who he was. He taught them. He embraced them. He loved all people equally. He showed them grace and extended a hand of comfort and loving correction. And you and I are called to do the same. Regardless of our interpretation of the biblical text, we cannot ignore or push aside Jesus' call to love our neighbors *and* our enemies. We can show love without compromising our convictions.

I've always found a sense of joy and purpose about this call to love radically when I read Mark 2:13-17, where we find Jesus dining with sinners—in fact, what some translations label "disreputable sinners." We can easily miss the scandalous nature of what's happening here. The religious leaders could not believe that Jesus, a rabbi—a holy man like themselves!— would dare spend time breaking bread, an intimate and holy experience, with people they considered sinners.

> Jesus went out to the lakeshore again and taught the crowds that were coming to him. As he walked along, he saw Levi son of Alphaeus sitting at his tax collector's booth. "Follow me and be my disciple," Jesus said to him. So Levi got up and followed him.
>
> Later, Levi invited Jesus and his disciples to his home as dinner guests, along with many tax collectors and other disreputable sinners. (There were many people of this kind among Jesus'

followers.) But when the teachers of religious law who were Pharisees saw him eating with tax collectors and other sinners, they asked his disciples, "Why does he eat with such scum?"

When Jesus heard this, he told them, "Healthy people don't need a doctor—sick people do. I have come to call not those who think they are righteous, but those who know they are sinners."

People who call themselves Christ followers should find themselves in this kind of situation: clinging to the love of Christ as we practically express his love to the world around us. More than we'd like to admit, we Christians can find ourselves more like the religious leaders than like Jesus—we get this crazy idea that we are too good to be spending time with broken people or that we ourselves are without a speck of sin and failure. It's mind-blowing. I understand the desire to avoid the negative influences of the world, but that doesn't give us the excuse to ignore the commandment and mission as a Christian to love the broken and hurting. Somebody once went out of his way to love each one of us, so why do we think the people around us deserve any less? We are called to be examples of Jesus to those around us so they may come to know the Love that placed itself on a cross for us.

For me, the most powerful part of this story in Mark is found in verse 17: "Healthy people don't need a doctor—sick people do. I have come to call not those who think they are righteous, but those who know they are sinners." In a bold and simple statement, Jesus debunks the idiotic remarks of the religious leaders, reminding them who needs Jesus' love. The reality is, everyone does.

This story really should make us question whether we are doing all we can to exude the love of God to those who need to see it. Are we spending time with people who are different from us? Are we opening our homes, our hearts, and our arms to people who may be a little rough around the edges but are still human and in need of compassion? It's really easy for us to justify why we shouldn't, but there are one hundred reasons more as to why we should.

Are you getting outside your comfort zone, or are you staying hidden in your Christian bubble and making justifications as to why you shouldn't?

Don't Withhold Love

Ultimately, Jesus' rule book for loving others boils down to this:

> "Love the Lord your God with all your heart and with all your soul and with all your mind and with all your strength." The second is this: "Love your neighbor as yourself." There is no commandment greater than these.
>
> MARK 12:30-31, NIV

Don't miss this: Jesus never said to love only people who are easy to love. He tells us simply to love.

Every time I open up the Bible, I cannot help but notice the number of times God commands us to love the people around us. We're told to love our enemies, our neighbors, our spouses, and the world alike. But while the Bible is pretty crystal clear that we should relentlessly love those we come across daily, it seems we often try to justify why we don't need to show love the way Jesus intended us to.

I've heard everything from "But he might think I'm affirming his actions" to "She's just not a nice person." But no justification gives us the right to withhold love from anyone, let alone from those who are broken and in need of it the most. The love of Jesus has no bounds, no limits, and no expectations. It just loves. If you call yourself a Christ follower, then you are called to reflect the same image with the same intensity. Love can take us places hate could never reach. Withholding love is withholding Jesus. It's possible to show love to those who are different from us without compromising core convictions.

You want people to see Jesus when they see you, even when you oppose their thoughts or ideals. You want people to find comfort in your presence, forgiveness in your heart, and love in your soul. You want people to know they can confide in you without being brashly criticized and judged irrationally. Jesus is pretty clear in what he says in the lines of Mark 12:31—the importance of love, especially when it comes to your neighbor: "The second is this: 'Love your neighbor as yourself.' There is no commandment greater than these" (NIV).

Pastors, teachers, brothers, and sisters, we are called to love all people in the name of Jesus. We are called to show compassion to those who need it. We are called to befriend those who are different from us, all to exude the grace and mercy of our Savior, Jesus. It may be messy, but it's our calling.

My life is filled with people who are different from me, have different beliefs than I do, see various parts of the Bible differently than I do, struggle with different sins than I do, hold to different core convictions than I do. Does this mean I keep quiet in fear of offending someone? No. Does loving someone mean you live a life of passivity? Nope. Love simply means you evaluate the way you say things and make sure they are said with compassion and mercy, even if they are contrary to the beliefs of others. It hurts my heart to see how many pastors and leaders are wrongfully handling conversations on certain controversial topics, and I believe that coming back to a heart of compassion is what's needed most. So many people are handling these conversations correctly, and I wish more people would follow suit in the name of Jesus.

Regardless of what side of a conversation you find yourself on, the commandment to love people and share truth in a loving way remains the same. We can exude love even when expressing our differences of opinion on topics such as marriage, immigration, and politics. But as we do, we must ask ourselves what it looks like to love the other person even in disagreement. I know this isn't always an easy task, but it's definitely an honorable one for all Christians who are willing to pick up their crosses daily. We're called to love people no matter where they are from, what they're doing, or how messed up they really are. You can still love people without approving of their decisions or way of life. You can speak truth but still do it in a loving and compassionate way. How do I know this? Because Jesus did this all throughout Scripture.

> Jesus returned to the Mount of Olives, but early the next morning he was back again at the Temple. A crowd soon gathered, and he sat down and taught them. As he was speaking, the teachers of religious law and the Pharisees brought a woman who had been caught in the act of adultery. They put her in front of the crowd.
>
> "Teacher," they said to Jesus, "this woman was caught in the act of adultery. The law of Moses says to stone her. What do you say?"
>
> They were trying to trap him into saying something they could use against him, but Jesus stooped down and wrote in the dust with his finger. They kept demanding an answer, so he stood up again and said, "All right, but let the one who has never sinned throw the first stone!" Then he stooped down again and wrote in the dust.

When the accusers heard this, they slipped
away one by one, beginning with the oldest, until
only Jesus was left in the middle of the crowd with
the woman. Then Jesus stood up again and said to
the woman, "Where are your accusers? Didn't even
one of them condemn you?"

"No, Lord," she said.

And Jesus said, "Neither do I. Go and sin no
more."

JOHN 8:1-11

This story is so powerful. Jesus loved this woman, just as he
loves people today who have sinned, and he longs for them to
turn to him. Although Jesus wasn't supporting the actions of
this woman, he still protected her from the hands of those who
were looking to stone her. His relentless love even goes out of
its way to protect us in the midst of our brokenness.

We Love, God Changes

I remember when I first became a believer in Jesus. I somehow thought it was my duty to change people for the sake
of spreading the gospel. I would rejoice when people would
find hope in Christ but would feel like a failure when someone would decline the invitation to know Jesus as Lord and
Savior. It was a little discouraging. But that's because my
understanding of how God works in my life was off.

I say this because I believe many of today's Christians put too much pressure on themselves to bring people to Jesus. It's our job to love people, not change them. Only the Holy Spirit has the power and authority to do such a thing. Our calling is to simply share the gospel in love and truth, showing the character of Jesus through our everyday lives. When you let yourself off the hook for being solely responsible for somebody's soul, you will find a totally new sense of freedom: the freedom to love. You don't have to be perfect. You don't have to know all the right things to say. You don't have to have all the answers. And if your message is totally rejected . . . it's not on you. It's between that individual and God. Maybe you'll get another opportunity to try, but it's not your job to change him or her.

Our job is to simply be available for those who are looking to know more about God, take opportunities to be vocal about our personal relationships with him, and continue to point people back to God with every question they may have. I didn't understand this in the early years of my faith, and I put way too much pressure on myself when it came to people being transformed. Why? Because we live in a performance-based culture, and yes, even pastors have a tendency to fall captive to its pull.

Like me, you probably feel pressured from multiple angles. We're told by advertising that we need to be attractive, by parents that we need good jobs, by teachers that we need good grades, by friends that we need to give more time. Jesus isn't like that. He doesn't make irrational demands and point a finger at us for not living up to the expectation. The only thing Jesus wants from us is our love. And when we learn to offer him that love, we long to obey him and live in the better way he has for us as well. It's a beautiful thing.

As we learned from Jesus in Matthew 25, we can love God simply by loving others. Whether that love produces a change in their lives is up to God. We don't have to stress about it. Only the Holy Spirit has the power and authority to change someone's heart. Our calling is to simply share the gospel in love and truth, showing the character of Jesus through our everyday lives. This alone is the calling of a Christian. This alone is a weighty yet fulfilling purpose for all who choose to pick up their crosses daily.

If we were to scour the Bible, we'd see there isn't a single passage that states we are called to change people ourselves. Why? Because it's not our job, and it was never intended to be. We must take a step back and realize that God's job is to be God and our job is to lead people toward the door that is hope. Once we've done this, we must let go and allow the one who created the world to take care of the rest. If we had the power to change people, the transformative love of God wouldn't be needed.

Don't waste your time trying to change people. Instead, focus on loving well.

Chapter 12

L O V E *is* M E S S Y

True love is a safe haven from the foul critics of the world, the cutting words, the judgments, and the ill-thought opinions. True love is an umbrella for others when it rains hurt, a warm hug in times of distress, and a shield for the oncoming arrows of darkness. If we truly want to love people well, we must open our hearts and our homes to be safe havens for those who are in need. We must allow them the opportunity to show their messiness. It's truly a beautiful thing, and I've seen it firsthand.

Over the last few years, my wife and I have taken this reality to heart. We believe that one of God's biggest callings on our life is to be a safe place, a refuge, for those who are in need. And this doesn't just go for the people we may easily identify as broken or needy in the world—because all of us are broken and needy, even if we appear the opposite. Juli and I have been allowed to act as a haven for people the world might think of as "having it all" but who in fact simply needed a place to feel safe and at home. Professional athletes, bestselling authors, top-charting musicians, and even some people you've seen in movies and television. We always make it a point to let people know we don't really care about who the world sees them as or what they do for a living. Because we're not here to get anything from them like most of the people they encounter, but instead, we want to see how we can be a blessing to them. We just care about who they are on the inside. As Christians, we shouldn't view people as media and society portray them to be. We should be a place for people to be the real, honest, authentic versions of themselves. What matters is someone's soul and heart—who he or she is when all the extra stuff is stripped away.

We are called to be safe havens for people. For my wife and me, this looks like opening ourselves up to be there in times of need—to be a place where people can fully drop their guards and be themselves without judgment. I can't begin to explain how many real and raw conversations we've had in our living room. Discussions about broken relationships, struggling marriages, faith, God, doubt, family dynamics, depression. No one feels the pressure to pretend to have it all together. That's not real life. And true love doesn't put that pressure on people.

And before we ever ask people to share about themselves, my wife and I give them "the gift of going second." We believe sharing our flaws and imperfections first gives people the time and opportunity to drop their guards and realize that they aren't the only people who are imperfect. For example, when I took my antidepressants in front of the crowd (chapter 2); it's so simple and yet has such a beautiful impact.

Jon Acuff said this about the gift of going second:

> When you go first, you give everyone in your
> church or your community or your small group or
> your blog, the gift of going second.
>   It's so much harder to be first. No one knows
> what's off limits yet and you're setting the boundaries
> with your words. You're throwing yourself on the
> honesty grenade and taking whatever fall out that
> comes with it. Going second is so much easier. And
> the ease only grows exponentially as people continue
> to share. But it has to be started somewhere.
> Someone has to go first and I think it has to be us.[17]

Usually when we do this, people are shocked. Responses such as "Wow! Didn't expect you guys to be so open with me" are fairly common in our house. Normally we respond with "We know! That's why we opened up." People don't expect others to be open, and that's why the world is in such a wounded place to begin with. If we all opened up more about our trials, imperfections, and flaws, we could come together in more profound ways in love and community. We've said this before, but it's worth saying again: It's okay to not be okay, regardless of what the world might try to impress on you.

I remember the first time I experienced this. A close friend and mentor began sharing about the current downfalls in his life, opening up about his marriage, a previously failed business, doubt, a struggle with anxiety, and that his past was filled with hard things. He opened up to me in a way I cannot begin to explain. It was as though he handed me the deepest and darkest secrets of his soul.

This was someone I looked up to immensely. I aspired to be like this man, and I couldn't believe he was telling me how broken and painful his life was. Part of me wondered why he'd share them with me. What if my views of him changed once he admitted his pain and imperfection? What if I didn't want to look up to him anymore? What if I responded in the exact opposite way from how he thought I'd respond? He didn't care. He wasn't worried about any of that. He wanted to be open and honest with me because that's what true leadership and love is all about. Love cannot exist without authenticity and transparency, and he modeled this so beautifully. Many leaders—many people—try to keep a composure of perfection. And one day I realized that I, too, was slowly turning into that kind of person, believing the lies that suggested I had to have it all together in order to lead well, love well, and influence well. This isn't the case at all. The world's greatest influence can be found through dirty, rotten, and brutal honesty. Those who exhibit this type of honesty are the people whom people like to follow. Those are the people whom you and I can relate to. Those are the people who are going to do big things in the world. I learned this really quickly.

So now, when we invite people over to our house, we

don't try to impress for the sake of impressing. Instead we just act ourselves, watching movies on the couch and making fun of our dogs as they run around and chase after our kids. Love doesn't have to be impressive to connect with people; it just needs to be authentic.

Love can be an outspoken, a messy, and a public display of affection—and it can display itself through quiet and intimate conversations in your living room. But above all, love should be a safe haven for anyone in our lives, no matter who they are or what they do. Just be a person where others can find rest.

The Son We Never Met

When my wife and I were first married, we lived in a one-bedroom apartment in Memphis, Tennessee, and it only cost us around $450 a month! The only downside was that it was in a not-so-nice part of the city, and it was fairly common to find shotgun shells and 9mm casings by our parking spot. But we were just happy to be together in a place we could call our own, no matter how unsafe it might have been.

Juli and I often walked around the apartment complex—we didn't have much money, so spending time outside was the cheapest way for us to have some fun. We'd talk about life, our future goals as a couple, the house we hoped to buy one day, and the dream of starting a little family. Our walks eventually turned into bike rides after we had saved up enough to buy those little bikes. Mine was some hipster version of a fixie, and Juli was sporting her beach cruiser with a small basket on the front. (We tried to put our dog in the basket a few times, but she wasn't too keen on it.) We had a blast and spent a lot of time riding around together.

One day while we were riding our normal route, we spotted a young girl playing in the grass of a common area outside our apartment. We noticed that there weren't any adults around—and she was so little—so we asked if she needed anything.

"Hi! What's your name?" Juli asked.

"My name is Annie," the girl said.

"Do your parents know you're out here?" I asked her. Annie put a hand on her hip, shook the two pigtails on her head, and said with a touch of sass, "They sure do!"

"Okay!" Juli and I laughed. "Have a good day! Be safe."

But just as we started to pedal off into the distance, we heard a faint "Wait! Wait!" We turned around and found the little girl running toward us. She asked if she could walk around with us. "Sure!" Juli told her. "But go ask your mom first."

"She won't care," she said and began following us no matter what we said or did. We asked what her favorite things to do were and whether she had any brothers or sisters. Little did we know that our walk around the neighborhood with her would turn into a routine. Whenever we'd make our way outside, we'd see the same little girl in the distance, waving at us and excited to join us. Some days we rode bikes and other days we just walked the dog, but no matter what, this Memphis-raised girl would join us every step of the way.

One day Annie ran toward us in excitement and shouted, "Do you want to meet my mom?"

"Of course we do!" Juli said. "Your mom is probably wondering who these crazy people are you keep telling her about."

We made our way to another part of the apartment complex and saw a somber-looking woman sitting on the curb underneath a carport, staring at her phone. Annie ran up to her, smiling from ear to ear. "Momma! This is Jerry and Julian—they're the ones I walk with who have the really cute dog." We didn't bother correcting her with our real names—we'd tried time and time again, but she insisted that she would only call us Jerry and Julian.

"It's nice to meet you! My name is Elaine," Annie's mother said, stretching out her hand to shake mine.

"Yeah! Nice to meet you, too," I said. "Your daughter is quite the character. We enjoy her company on our walks. She's welcome to come with us anytime."

"Thank you," Elaine said, struggling to stand and brush off the back of her pants. She was obviously pregnant.

"Congratulations on the baby," I said with a big smile. And the response I got was something I didn't expect.

"Yeah, but Momma is going to go get that thing out of her tomorrow," Annie said.

"Annie!" Elaine shook her head. "Why would you say that? I don't even know these people. I'm so sorry, you guys."

"Sorry, Momma," Annie said.

Juli and I looked at each other. We knew what Annie had meant. Her mom was heading out to get an abortion, which meant this sweet little baby boy or girl wouldn't get to live. We said our good-byes and started to head back home, but Juli stopped me halfway there and said, "Jarrid, we need to tell that woman we will help her if she chooses to keep the baby."

"What?" I said. "She doesn't know us. Why would she trust anything we say to her?"

My wife has a lot more faith during uncertainty than I do. But something within me knew that what Juli was saying was the right thing to do. We don't believe in abortion under any circumstances. But we also don't believe anybody has the right to tell someone not to get an abortion without personally offering assistance before, during, and after the birth. Love offers wisdom and then the follow-up to make it happen. Love walks alongside people through all kinds of situations. Love gives people the comfort of knowing they are not alone, even during times of uncertainty and doubt.

So picture this, if you will: Jarrid Wilson, tall, skinny white man, riding a hipster fixie bike back to the carport to tell a woman he'd just met that if she didn't have an abortion, he and his wife would do anything to help her. Seem crazy? Yup. Every bit of crazy, but that's what love does. Elaine looked at me as though I was insane. Because in reality, I was. But something within her seemed to change, and after exchanging phone numbers in case she changed her mind, Juli and I received a text from her saying that she wouldn't have the abortion if we were really serious about helping her. And we were.

The next few months would be some of the craziest months of our lives. Doctor appointments, hospital visits, ultrasounds, prenatal vitamins, baby shopping, and more. Elaine was a single mom, alone, with little-to-no financial stability, and in need of love and some encouragement to get through the hardships of life. We eventually got her connected with an adoption agency, moved her into an apartment of her own, away from an abusive situation, and helped get Annie enrolled back in school. She hadn't been in more than three years. We wanted to do everything we could to help this little family that had been abandoned by the father and left out in the cold. We weren't trying to be heroes. We just wanted to show them love. Even though we didn't know what we were doing, we knew that we were called to love no matter what that looked like or cost. And somehow God kept providing the finances we needed to take care of ourselves and this little family that had come into our lives.

Looking back, we really were crazy to try to do something like this so early on in our marriage. Many of our friends and even some of our family didn't really get it. Was it truly the right choice for us to barge into someone's life like this? But that's the beauty of love: It does crazy things in the name of compassion and support. Love isn't always comfortable, and it doesn't always make sense. But it's still love, and it's always worth the effort.

In the midst of helping Elaine and her unborn child, I ended up taking a job that required us to move across the country. It was a great opportunity for Juli and me to venture to a new part of the country together, make a good living for ourselves, and progress in our relationship with each other. Obviously, one of the only things holding us back was that we had promised to help with Elaine's pregnancy in any way that we could, but we quickly realized we could do that even if we were living a few thousand miles away. Elaine agreed because she planned on moving to Texas with some family anyway. We would continue to pay for her apartment and send money each month for food and basic necessities. And we eventually got her approved for a system in Tennessee that would take care of all her hospital bills. God continued to pave the way to help out this little family, and Elaine and Annie quickly became part of our own. Even after we moved, we celebrated birthdays, called each other weekly, and welcomed ultrasound photos.

Then late one night in the winter of 2012, we got a call that changed everything. This wasn't a normal time for Elaine to call, so right off the bat Juli thought something might have happened. Elaine explained to Juli that after lots of prayer and consideration, she wanted us to adopt the baby. Elaine felt as though it would be the best thing for her to do given her current situation, and she didn't want the baby to be adopted by anyone but us.

We immediately knew our answer.

"Yes."

We knew we were still early into our marriage, but something about this little baby being in our family felt right. We'd been there for so much of the journey that adopting this little baby—a boy, we now knew—seemed like the perfect ending to such an incredible story. And did I mention that a few weeks prior to hearing from Elaine, Juli received news from her doctor that having children of our own would be nearly impossible? This whole thing had God written all over it.

The next few months leading up to the baby's birth were filled with having conversations with lawyers, preparing for house visits, raising money to pay for the private adoption fees, and getting our house ready for the arrival of a newborn. People thought we were crazy. But we knew God had opened a door for us to bring life into our home, and we were so thankful for the opportunity. We knew it would be tough. We knew adoption would bring its own struggles. And we knew that adopting a child of a different ethnicity would stir up interesting conversations. But we didn't care. Those things didn't worry us one bit. All we knew was that a child needed a home, and we were more than willing to open up our hearts to be available.

One month before the baby was due, Elaine called us, wondering if giving up the baby was the right thing for her to do. We told her, "That is completely up to you, Elaine! Our hearts would be so full if you decided to keep your little boy, but please know we're also open to giving him a loving home with us if you so choose. We want what you want."

I could see a little disappointment in Juli's eyes as we talked to Elaine, and I knew how she felt. Over the last four months, we had been preparing for this little boy, and we had even already chosen his name. But our disappointment was not out of selfishness. Our goal from the very beginning had been that this mother would choose to give her child life. We were sad knowing we might not be welcoming him into our family, but we knew God had a wonderful plan. We couldn't let her decision, regardless of what it was, cover up the beauty of a mother choosing to let her little baby have life.

As the phone call came to an end, I could see tears in Juli's eyes. Juli said we'd be here for Elaine no matter what she decided.

That was the last time we ever heard from Elaine. We don't know what happened to the baby boy, but we pray daily that he is safe, joyful, and living a fulfilling life with his momma. God's plan may not have been for us to adopt that baby, but God showed us something valuable about love. What would we do if we were given the opportunity to help someone in need? How would we respond if an opportunity to love someone was plastered right in our faces? Would we make excuses because of our age, financial situation, and lack of faith, or would we instead be bold and courageous, knowing that God would take care of everything if we just made ourselves available to the need at hand?

We may have never met the little boy we planned on welcoming into our home, but that doesn't mean our time was wasted. In fact, I believe what happened was God's plan from the very beginning. Our job was to follow his lead and love where we could, exuding a light and an aroma of compassion.

Loving others isn't always going to be easy. And just because you are following God's direction doesn't mean everything is going to go the way you planned. We have to look at the bigger picture. God is in complete control— our only job is to make ourselves available to love people who are in need. That's such a big and beautiful part of the Christian life that so many people seem to forget. Following Jesus is about God loving you, you loving God, and you loving people in the name of God.

Every day we will have opportunities to breathe out love onto people who are in need, hurting, and broken. We should not beg God to use us and then ignore the opportunities to love the people in front of us. Being used by God doesn't always mean doing what we perceive as "big" things. Being used by God means taking every opportunity, no matter how big or small, and truly investing our time and energy into them.

A Final Word

This journey into living in God's love will take the rest of our lives. His love for us doesn't change, but our understanding of that love and how we show it to others will be constantly growing and changing. So as we reach the end of this book,

I want you to hold on to this: The God who created the heavens and the earth loved you enough to create you in his own image. He didn't have to do this, but he wanted to. Your existence is so intrinsically beautiful. You were made with love, made unique, made for a purpose, and destined to share God's love with everyone you come across. Because after all, we love because God first loved us. Once we truly breathe it in, we cannot help but breathe it out upon the world around us. We love because God is love, which means that, as redeemed people reflecting his image, *we* are meant to be living, breathing ambassadors of love. If we seek to discover and live out his love daily, we won't regret it. God's love is oxygen for our souls, and as we breathe in the rhythm of his love, our lives will never be the same.

NOTES

1. "Suicide: Facts at a Glance," Centers for Disease Control and Prevention, 2015, accessed February 24, 2017, https://www.cdc.gov /violenceprevention/pdf/suicide-datasheet-a.pdf.
2. Matthew Henry, *Short Comments on Every Chapter of the Holy Bible* (London: The Religious Tract Society, 1839), 992.
3. Eugene H. Peterson, *A Long Obedience in the Same Direction: Discipleship in an Instant Society* (Downers Grove, IL: InterVarsity, 2000), 29.
4. *Oxford Living Dictionaries*, s.v. "prodigal," https://en.oxforddictionaries .com/definition/us/prodigal.
5. Rick Warren, *The Purpose Driven Life* (Grand Rapids, MI: Zondervan, 2012), 38.
6. Alexander Maclaren, *Expositions of Holy Scripture: The Epistles General of I and II Peter and I John* (New York: A. C. Armstrong and Son, 1910), 347.
7. Eugene H. Peterson, *Run with the Horses: The Quest for Life at Its Best* (Downers Grove, IL: InterVarsity, 2009), 150.
8. Elisabeth Elliot, "Elisabeth Elliot Quotes," Goodreads, accessed March 3, 2017, http://www.goodreads.com/quotes/298278.
9. Henry David Thoreau, *The Portable Thoreau* (New York: Penguin Books, 2012), 454.
10. Jarrid Wilson, "I'm Dating Someone Even Though I'm Married," *Jarrid Wilson,* January 6, 2014, http://jarridwilson.com/im-dating-someone-even -though-im-married/.
11. A. W. Tozer, *The Pursuit of God* (Abbotsford, WI: Aneko Press, 2015), 4.

12. D. L. Moody, *The Overcoming Life* (Orlando, FL: Bridge-Logos, 2007), 336.

13. Samuel Chadwick, *The Way to Pentecost* (Fort Washington, PA: CLC Publications, 2013), 6.

14. "From Death to Life," YouTube video, posted by FromDeathToLifeVideo, November 28, 2011, https://youtu.be/xSJ8Nfov6C4.

15. "The Power of Forgiveness," YouTube video, posted by CBS, June 7, 2011, https://www.youtube.com/watch?v=o2BITY-3Mp4.

16. Francis Chan, *Crazy Love: Overwhelmed by a Relentless God* (Colorado Springs, CO: David C Cook, 2013), 23.

17. Jon Acuff, "Confessing 'Safe Sins,'" *Stuff Christians Like*, March 4, 2009, accessed February 24, 2017, http://stuffchristianslike.net/2009/03/04/502 -confessing-safe-sins-2.

ABOUT THE AUTHOR

Jarrid Wilson is a husband, a dad, a pastor, an author, an inspirational blogger, and the founder of Anthem of Hope. He is the author of *Jesus Swagger*, *Wondrous Pursuit*, *30 Words*, and *Love Is Oxygen*.

His articles have been viewed by tens of millions, showcased on some of today's hottest talk shows, and featured on national news stations worldwide. He is a dynamic speaker whose outside-the-box perspectives have gained him national recognition from some of today's most influential Christian leaders and pastors.

His highly unconventional way of sharing faith takes a fresh look at the way Jesus would call individuals to live out their everyday lives. Unafraid to tackle tough and controversial topics, Jarrid is known for his refreshing perspectives on what others may view as set in black and white. His blog is one of the most talked about faith-based blogs on the web, and his dedication to showcase the relentless love of Jesus has been paramount to his success as a writer and leader.

Jarrid and his wife, Juli, live in Nashville, Tennessee, with their sons, Finch and Denham, and their dog, Eloise.